Asia's Financial Industry

1986 – 2016

Asia's Financial Industry 1986 – 2016

A Custodian's Perspective

Lawrence Au

YOUCAXTON PUBLICATIONS
OXFORD & SHREWSBURY

ISBN 978-191117-541-4
Printed and bound in Great Britain.
Published by YouCaxton Publications 2016

YouCaxton Publications
enquiries@youcaxton.co.uk

To all the professionals in the custody industry

in Asia and across the world

This book is dedicated to:

My wife Kamshing

for all her support and encouragement

&

My daughters, Joyce and Joelle,

for the life experience as their father

Contents

Illustrations

Prologue

It all started in 1993 when the Chase Manhattan Bank approached me for a job in custody. That was the first time I had come across custody as a defined financial business line even though I had been in the banking industry for already ten years at that time.

The term global custody was commonly acknowledged to be invented by Doug Bonnar of the Chase Manhattan Bank. In 1974, the Ford Foundation in the U.S. appointed four international fund managers to diversify its assets and earn foreign income, but it was keen to separate management from administration and looked to Chase to provide safekeeping and settlement services. Bonnar, the trust and investment manager for Chase in the U.K., was tasked with the challenge. He and his team put together an arrangement of services that he called 'global custody' for providing to the Ford Foundation out of Chase's London Branch.

Inside Chase, however, the credit for creating and nurturing the global custody business actually went to Colin Grimmsey who worked for Bonnar. Grimsey successfully lobbied the Securities & Exchange Commission for an exemption to allow Chase to hold foreign assets in its foreign bank branches on behalf of US mutual funds. They were the first investor segment in the U.S. diversifying internationally. Then the 1974 Employee Retirement Income Security Act (ERISA) was introduced, and US pension plans followed the same path. From then on, global custody has evolved and transformed into a multi-billion-Dollar industry today.

The custody industry in the Asia Pacific region was in its infancy in the 1990's. There were many more players than today, including names such as Barclays, Bankers Trust, Morgan Stanley, and

Bank of America that are no longer in the business today. Chase, State Street, Citibank, Deutsche Bank, and Morgan Guaranty Trust were the key global players, while Hong Kong & Shanghai Bank, Standard Chartered Bank, and Bank of Bermuda were key local and regional players.

I had very minimal prior experience in custody and had no idea what the business was all about. However, the head of Chase's Global Investor Services for the APAC region at that time, Mark Huber, was convinced by my experience as a regional correspondent banker and believed they could train me on the custody product knowledge. Indeed, Chase was the training ground for the whole custody industry at that time. Chase alums were found in senior roles in almost every single major custodian bank in the initial years of the industry's development in the region and globally.

I joined Chase as the regional sales manager for Asia. My colleague at Chase covering the sales in Australia and New Zealand was Laurence Bailey who subsequently became my counterpart at JP Morgan as head of Asia Pacific for its Global Investor Services. KK Tse was the regional sales manager for Asia at State Street and Leow Chong-Jin was the regional sales manager for Asia at Citibank at that time. The four of us were the local talent who started about the same time in the early 90's. We worked in the industry for close to three decades in the following years and headed the business for our respective banks in the region.

The *Global Custodian* magazine has the following comment on the custody industry on its website: It's [custody] not rocket science. It doesn't save lives, and no one from the industry is going to win a Nobel Prize. Yet still they flock out of the world's top business schools and universities to tackle issues such as pan-European transfer agency and net asset value calculations. The talent pool in the business has always been impressive.... [1]

So what is it about the custody business that has kept me and others going for almost our entire careers in the industry?

To me, it has been an amazing journey over the past twenty-four years.

Firstly, custody has come a long way since the days of ensuring client's bonds and share certificates were safely locked away in a bank vault. The *Financial Times* described the custody industry in the early 1990's as the 'sleepy backwater' of international banking. However, the rapid advance of technology and scripless trading, together with globalisation, asset diversification, innovation in investment strategies, regulatory changes, and the quest for scale, efficiency and disappearing margins have continuously pushed custodians up the value chain to offer services that are very far and beyond the scope and sophistication level that custodians started out with.

There has never been a dull moment during the past twenty-four years finding my path in the sleepy backwater. I have been learning new things every day, and there are still many new things for me to learn even having been in the industry for twenty-four years.

Secondly, the industry has gone through many consolidations. The sheer size of continuous investment required to stay in the competition has been pushing the exit of many former heavyweights. I spent only one year at Chase and joined Morgan Guaranty Trust (MGT) in 1994, the original House of Morgan founded by John Pierpont Morgan. However, the experience came to a premature halt when MGT sold the global custody business with US$2,100 billion in AUM to The Bank

1 *Definition & History: History of the Industry*, http://www.globalcustody.net/industry_history/ : 27 April 2015

of New York in 1995, which was at that time a completely domestic custodian bank headquartered in Wall Street in New York. In the same stroke, the local custody business in Europe with US$600 billion in AUM was sold by MGT to Banque Paribas headquartered in Paris. The decision was justified on the grounds that substantial investment in technology would be required to remain a leader. In the banking world, MGT was held as the role model at the time in transforming from a commercial bank into an investment bank. The continuous investment into the low-margin business of custody was not deemed the best use of the bank's capital resources.

Morgan Guaranty Trust Headquarter Building at 23 Wall Street; Source: Wikipedia

Then a year later, Barclays - Britain's largest custodian - sold its custody unit to Morgan Stanley citing the same reasons. Then two years later in 1998, Morgan Stanley sold the custody business to Chase. The musical chairs have continued over the past three decades. Indeed, many global names came to the region and then went down Memory Lane including Chase (which changed its name to JP Morgan after the merger of the two banks), Bank of America, Chemical Bank, RBS Trust, Midland, NatWest, Bankers Trust, Dresdner Bank, Deutsche Global Custody, Bank of Bermuda, and Mellon Trust.

In this process of industry consolidation and evolution, I have had the privilege of being given the opportunity of building the custody businesses for Bank of New York, Northern Trust, and BNP Paribas from ground level as each started out in the region. Each institution came with its strengths and unique challenges. It has given me immense pleasure to have been a pioneering contributor to their successes today.

Thirdly, the custody industry has grown so significantly bigger today. Oliver Wyman estimated in its yearly Securities Services Report that the total assets under custody by the top ten global custodians amounted to over US$140 trillion at end of 2013 and the total revenues generated by the top ten custodians were between US$9-10 billion. I cannot find any official figures, but would guess that in 1993 the equivalent AUM would probably be less than US$14 trillion only!

Custody is an annuity business that provides a stream of fee-based income and net interest income to the banks with very sticky client relationships that often go on for fifteen to twenty years and beyond if client satisfaction is consistently maintained. In the new era of Basel III, this line of business is even more important as a key contributor of liquidity supporting other businesses within the banking group.

Since the global financial crisis in 2008, many social and economic faults have been blamed on the greed of bankers. The true value of banking has been seriously questioned. As custodians, we are quietly playing a fundamental but very important role for institutions and individuals day in and day out. We protect the assets of pension funds, mutual funds, and the precious investments of individuals and institutions by maintaining clear segregation of assets to identify ownership throughout the entire investment chain. We are responsible for ensuring smooth and secure settlement of financial transactions for our clients, and maintaining accurate records for all the financial assets entrusted to us worldwide.

While no one from the custody industry is going to win a Nobel Prize, we, as an industry, are fully embedded in the very core of real economy banking that has been quietly creating value to society.

To me, that's not a bad deal.

1. What to Safekeep?

A fundamental question that puzzled me when I first started in the custody industry was: what exactly do we safekeep?

The Oxford Dictionary defines the word custodian as a person that protects or takes care of something or someone. For example, the responsibilities of the custodian of a museum are to ensure the safety, upkeep an inventory of the art displayed or stored by the museum.

While the core function of a custodian is safekeeping of assets, stocks and bonds are today traded and settled electronically and recorded as electronic book entries on the computer records of central depositories. Physical safekeeping has become very rare.

Before the computer age, buying and selling of shares and bonds would actually involve delivery and the changing hands of certificates in physical form. Custodian banks provide services to clients for keeping the share and bond certificates of clients locked in secure vaults, and making delivery of the securities certificates upon client's instruction. Safekeeping is a core function.

Thriving business at a bank's vault department; Source: postcard

Strongrooms were built in the basement of the bank where the ceilings were vaulted, hence the name. Vaults were an integral part of the bank's building within which they were built using armoured walls and a tightly fastened door closed with a complex lock.

Bank vaults were enormous structures built to customer orders. The vault was usually the most critical part of a new bank building to be designed and built. The architecture process would begin with the design of the vault and the rest of the bank was built around it. The vault manufacturer consulted with the bank to determine factors such as the total vault size, its desired shape, and the location of the door. Then the manufacturer configured the equipment to make the vault panels and door; the built vault would then be delivered and installed on site at the basement before the rest of the building process continued around and above it.

A search on the archives of global custodian banks will find many images of highly secure bank vaults with thick steel doors and sophisticated locks to ensure absolute safety.

An image of security; Source: postcard

Many of the terminologies that we are still using today in the investment industry had their origin in the days when securities were in physical forms.

In the early days, when a company or the government issued a bond to raise money, they would place advertisements in newspapers to attract potential investors for the bond issue. A prospectus would be printed together with application forms to be sent out to firms and individuals who had responded to the advertisements. *Scrip* or subscription receipts, would be sent out on receipt of deposit payments, and the bond itself only would be sent out when all instalments had been paid.

Each bond was printed with a sheet of coupons. The interest rate stated on the bond was called the *coupon rate* and *coupon payments* were typically paid out every six months. Bond owners literally had to *clip* out the next coupon on the sheet and present it to the bank or paying agent in exchange for the designated dividend payment. The method of processing the payments was very labour-intensive. The coupon number would be recorded in a ledger, the coupon cancelled, and counted into bundles for storage.

During the World Wars I & II, War Bonds were issued by the US government in large quantity to fund the wars. The bonds were denominated in small amounts, e.g. US$25, to encourage subscription by the mass population to instil patriotism. People could purchase a US$25 War Bond for US$18.75. The US government would take that money to help pay for tanks, planes, ships, uniforms, weapons, medicine, food and everything else the military needed to fight the war. Ten years from the time the War Bond was purchased, people could redeem it and get US$25 - hence the birth of *zero-coupon* bonds because these bonds were not issued with sheets of coupons for payments every six months.

Posters picturing Uncle Sam or soldiers on the battlefield were everywhere imploring the ordinary Americans to do their part. Children did their part too. Schools held their War Bond campaigns and children would bring in nickels and dimes and quarters to purchase 25 cents War Stamps to paste onto War Bond booklets. Competition among schools was fierce to see which one would raise most money.

An image of a War Bond poster; Source: WWII Museum New Orleans

As a result, War Bonds and War Stamps subscription-processing grew to involve a massive workload. Banks started to employ the widows of dead soldiers as cheap, temporary labour during the bond issuance and subscription periods.

Kids in school uniforms showing each other their War Stamp collections; war widows sitting in huge banking halls processing War Bond subscriptions... these became touching scenes in many old wartime Hollywood movies!

2. Engine of the Capitalist World

During the early 1990's, most securities were still traded in stock exchanges around the world using the open outcry auction system. It was only over the last two to three decades that securities have gradually been trading in an electronic environment in stock exchanges around the world as they are today.

Stock exchanges are truly the engine of the capitalist world as trillions of Dollars are traded through them every day.

Many historical sources suggest that exchanges grew out of trading in commodities and agricultural products. There were many early examples in Europe of markets that were similar to stock markets. In the 1100's, for example, France had a system where *courretiers de change* managed agricultural debts throughout the country on behalf of banks. This can be seen as the first major example of brokerage because these people effectively traded debts.

Later on, the merchants of Venice were credited with trading government securities as early as the 13th century, soon afterwards followed by their counterparts in other Italian cities of Pisa, Verona, Genoa, and Florence.

A number of European exchanges traced their origin to the 14th and 15th centuries: Antwerp Bourse, 1460; Lyons Bourse, 1506; Toulouse Bourse, 1549; Hamburg Bourse, 1558; and the London Royal Exchange, 1571. All these early exchanges had one thing missing: stocks. Although the infrastructure and institutions resembled today's stock exchanges, nobody was actually trading shares of a company. Instead, they dealt with the affairs of government, businesses, and individual debt. The system and organisation were similar, but the actual properties being traded were different.

The Amsterdam Stock Exchange, established in 1602, is generally regarded as the world's first stock exchange. It was established as a trading centre for the issuance of a newly formed joint stock company, the Dutch East India Company.

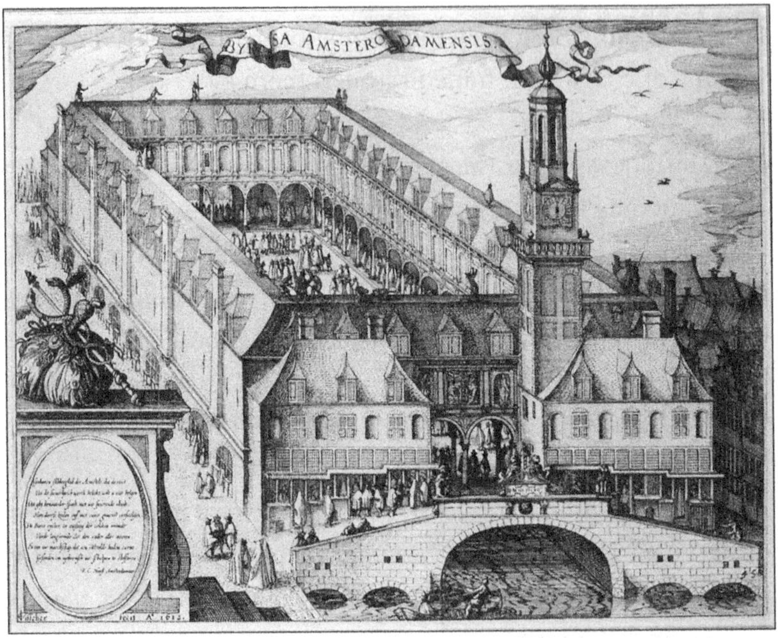

Amsterdam Stock Exchange in 1600's; Source: Wikipedia

When the East Indies was discovered to be a land of riches offering plenty of trade opportunities, explorers started to sail there in droves. However, voyages to the far corners of the globe in the East were highly risky, and many of these voyages did not make it home. Ships were lost; fortunes were squandered. Financiers realised they had to do something to mitigate all that risk. As a result, a unique, limited-liability company structure was developed. In 1600, the famous East India Company was formed in London and it was the first company to use this structure. These early investors realised that putting all their eggs into one basket was not a smart way to approach investment in East Indies trading. Instead of investing in a single voyage and risking the loss of all the money invested, investors would purchase shares in multiple companies so that even if one ship was lost out of three or four invested companies, the investor would still make a profit.

In 1602, the Dutch East India Company officially became the world's first publicly traded company when it released shares of the Company on the Amsterdam Stock Exchange. Stocks and bonds were issued to investors and each investor was entitled to a fixed percentage of East India Company profits. This company structure proved to be very successful and was the financial engine behind the Netherland's rise as a world power.

Within a decade, similar charters had been granted to other businesses throughout England, France, Belgium, and the Netherlands.

Stock exchanges in the early days were merely meeting places where investors met to buy and sell their stocks. The market did not take place in formal settings. The London Stock Exchange was said to trace its origin to 1773 when investors gathered in a coffee house in the City of London called Jonathan's Coffee House to conduct business. Early stocks were handwritten on sheets of paper, and investors traded these stocks with other investors in the coffee shop. Later, investors realised that the business would be more efficient if a dedicated marketplace was established where businessmen could trade stocks without yelling across a crowded café. In 1801, the London Stock Exchange was formally established in a new purpose-built building.

London Stock Exchange in 1810; Source: Wikipedia

Stocks became known as funds allocated by a company from its capital for the purpose of financial investment. Shares became known as equal parts into which a company's stocks were divided for purchase by individuals or other companies to become shareholders and as such becoming entitled to a proportion of the company's profits. Ordinary shares became known as equities.

These were radical and innovative concepts enabling the value of a company to be distributed in a way that was impossible before, and they provided much more robust means for growth.

An open outcry auction system was used whereby bids and offers were made open at the trading floor of the stock exchange giving all participants a chance to compete for the order with the best price. A method of communication soon evolved between traders on a stock exchange involving shouting and the use of hand signals to transfer information about buy and sell orders, which we see in old time photos and movies featuring stock exchanges.

Across the Atlantic, The New York Stock Exchange also had a humble beginning. In New York in 1792, a group of twenty-four most prominent brokers signed an agreement to meet at regular hours daily under an old buttonwood tree (American sycamore tree) on the Wall Street in Lower Manhattan, New York City, to buy and sell securities. This marked the beginning of the investment community of Wall Street.

Traders under the buttonwood tree; Source: Wikipedia

A century earlier, Dutch settlers had built a wall in Lower Manhattan to protect themselves. The path, where the banks of the East River joined those of the Hudson River on the west, had become a bustling business place and was named Wall Street. Early merchants built their warehouses and shops along it, together with the Federal Hall and a church. It was a popular place to buy and sell furs, tobacco, spices, molasses and gunpowder. Buyers and sellers of securities had also been meeting informally along it. New York was also the US national capital from 1785 until 1790; in fact George Washington was inaugurated on the steps of the Federal Hall on Wall Street.

On 17 May 1792, twenty-four brokers signed the 'Buttonwood Agreement' outside at 68 Wall Street, agreeing to trade exclusively among themselves on commission basis and not through the auctioneers. This formed the fundamental structure of the eventual New York Stock and Exchange Board formally established in 1817.

Incidentally, during the summer rout of the Chinese A-Share market in 2015, a private company 100% owned by the State Administration of Foreign Exchange (SAFE) called Buttonwood Investment Platform Ltd (*Wutongshu*), and its two fully-owned subsidiaries, were used as the vehicles to buy shares during its market intervention, as reported by the *Shanghai Securities News*. How this special-purpose entity got inspiration for its name from the Buttonwood Agreement has not been explained.

In any case, back to 1817, the initial offerings of the New York Stock and Exchange Board involved securities from five New York based companies. The first listed company on the New York Stock Exchange was the bank founded in 1784 by George Washington's Treasury Secretary, Alexander Hamilton, named The Bank of New York.

3. Bicycle Couriers

Before the 1990's, settlement of securities around the world would typically involve physical movements of paper instruments, certificates and transfer forms. Registrars or payment agents made payments by paper cheques after verifying that proper certificates and other requisite documents had been received.

It is a relatively recent phenomenon that securities are publicly traded and settled in electronic form.

Since the founding of the oldest formal stock exchange, Amsterdam Stock Exchange, in 1602, it had always taken a number of days after a trade transaction to complete final settlement due to physical delivery and settlement. This created the risk and uncertainty whether the trade would be completed on settlement day.

During the 1700's, the Amsterdam Stock Exchange established close links with the London Stock Exchange and they would often list each other's stocks (*cross-listings*). To clear the trades, time was required for the physical stock certificate or cash to move from Amsterdam to London and back. This led to the standard settlement period of fourteen days, which was the time it usually took for a courier to make the journey on horseback and by ship. Most exchanges continued to use the same settlement period over the next few hundred years until the advent of computer technology in the 1980's.

Physical delivery and settlement involved a lot of risk as well as manual workload and logistical challenges.

My first exposure to physical securities settlement practices was during the time I worked as a correspondent banker at Security

Pacific National Bank ('SecPac' for short by people in the industry). Headquartered in Los Angeles, SecPac became the fifth largest bank in the U.S. during the 1980's after several mergers and acquisitions. It had a sizable presence in Asia through a major stake in a local bank based in Hong Kong called the Bank of Canton, which was in its early days founded by Dr. Soong Tse-Ven, brother of the three Soong sisters, and the finance minister of the Kuomintang government.

SecPac's Hong Kong Office was on the top floor of the Bank of Canton Building at No 1 Queen's Road Central. On the walls of the board room, which was designed in oriental decor with antique Chinese furniture, were replicas of a number of war bonds issued by the Kuomintang government during the war times and signed by Dr. Soong.

In late 1988, SecPac acquired a specialist business in New York that offered clearing services of US government securities and Japanese government bonds, and changed its name to Secor. As the regional sales manager for SecPac's correspondent banking business in Asia, I made a trip to Japan for joint calls with the Secor securities clearing team to visit clients and discuss transferring their account and business to SecPac.

The Japanese economy was at its peak in the late 1980s. Japan exports had built up huge trade surpluses and the Yen had become very strong. The exchange rate of USD against Yen dropped half in two years from 254.11 in January 1885 to 128.25 in December 1987[2]. Japanese businessmen were buying up properties all over the world, especially in the U.S., including trophy properties such as movie studios (Universal Studios and Columbia Pictures in Los Angeles), famous golf courses (Pebble Beach in Monterey, North California)

2 Japanese Yen Historical Rates, Wikipedia

and iconic real estate (Rockefeller Center in New York). At the financial district of Marunouchi, a big billboard was erected to show the exchange rates of the Yen versus US Dollar minute by minute.

This exuberant economic confidence was epitomised in a book entitled *Japan as Number One: Lessons for America* written by Ezra Vogel, a Harvard academic, in which he portrayed Japan, with its strong economy and cohesive society, as the world's most dynamic industrial nation. Japan Inc. seemed ready to obliterate American industries from automakers to supercomputers. Case studies on Japanese leading companies such as Sony, Toyota, Mitsubishi, and Theory Z by Japanese American management guru, William Ouchi, were discussed and debated in MBA classes around the world.

Book cover of Japan as Number 1; Source: Wikipedia

The JGB (Japanese Government Bond) market was the second largest government debt market in the world during the 1980's. In 1987, the total outstanding volume of JGBs totaled 92 trillion Yen (approximately USD 717 billion), representing 43.7% of the GNP. Daily turnover in the JGB cash market averaged 2-3 trillion Yen and 7-8 trillion Yen during bull market. Up to 95% of this volume in OTC trades was being traded, cleared and settled in physical form among securities houses and banks. Moreover, they were coupon bonds with semi-annual interest payments.

A key challenge among the securities investment firms in Tokyo was how to deliver the physical securities to counter-parties on settlement date within the deadline. Bicycle couriers were typically employed to deliver these securities in central Tokyo in order to beat traffic congestion. Clad in bright racing jerseys, they flew through the central business districts, carrying documents entrusted to them for safe and speedy delivery.

A cool image of a Japanese bicycle courier; Source: Wikipedia

Bicycle couriers had originated around 1970 in New York City and had quickly become an icon of the city. They had made their first appearance in Tokyo in the 1980's making deliveries in Marunouchi, Otemachi, Chiyoda, Ginza, Akasaka - the financial and business districts around the Imperial Palace area. Traffic in Tokyo was notoriously jam-packed in the 1980's, but bicycle couriers could use the sidewalk or go up one-way streets, and they could choose the quickest route by nimbly avoiding traffic lights, making them the most effective means for delivery around Central Tokyo.

Sailing past motor vehicles on crowded streets, bicycle courier became a popular job among young people who saw the trade as a way to look good, feel good and stay in shape. Consequently, the messengers on the bikes were seen as 'cool' (of course this is a term in vogue only in recent years, but not at that time). Some of the messengers were die-hard cycling fans who took their jobs as an extension of their hobby; they wore outfits with eye-catching helmets, sunglasses, and messenger bags, and their unique fashions were featured in magazines.

The discussions at the meetings with the Japanese securities investment firms together with the Secor team were most entertaining. Besides service capabilities, fees and differentiation, a key aspect of the discussion was focused on the size and experience of the courier bicycle team, the routes it would cover to deliver the physical securities on the bike, and the logistics of such deliveries on a daily basis, rain or shine.

Physical delivery of securities gradually declined since Japanese bonds started to dematerialise in the late 1990's. However, bicycle couriers continued to develop into a kind of cult among young people in Japan. A movie called *Messengers* was shown in Japanese cinemas during the summer of 1999 - a little action-and-romance comedy. It was followed by a television series in autumn featuring the story of these bicycle couriers speeding through the traffic-clogged streets of central Tokyo. A boom was created among young people joining the trade of bicycle couriers.

In 2009, Tokyo hosted the Cycle Messenger World Championships, as well as the Bicycle Film Festival. It was reported that one Japanese cyclist finished third in one of the championship competitions!

4. An Accidental Innovation

The concept of a clearing house was an accidental innovation.

Until the early 1990's when the use of electronic payment systems was pushed globally, paper cheques were the primary means of payment other than cash.

Paper cheques are still widely used today in countries around the world for corporate and personal payments even though their usage is waning compared with electronic payments of millions of financial transactions valued in trillions of Dollars each day between sellers and purchasers of securities.

The cheque had its origins in the ancient banking system in which bankers would issue *bills of exchange* at the request of their customers to pay money to specified payees. This made trade so much easier by eliminating the need for merchants to carry large quantities of gold or silver to purchase goods and services.

It is not quite sure when the first cheques appeared. Some think the Romans may have invented the cheque about 352 B.C. but, even if that were true, the idea apparently didn't catch on. In the 13th century, the merchants of Venice developed the bill of exchange as a legal device to allow international trade without the need to carry large amounts of gold and silver but it probably wasn't until the early 1500's, in Holland, that the cheque first got common usage.

Amsterdam was a major international shipping and trading centre at that time. People who had accumulated cash began depositing it with Dutch *cashiers* for a fee as a safer alternative to keeping the money at home. Eventually the cashiers agreed to pay their depositors' debts out of the money in each account based on the depositor's written order or *note* to do so.

The concept soon spread to England and elsewhere. By the 17th century, bills of exchange were being used for domestic payments in England. A type of bill of exchange, called *drawn notes*, then began to evolve into an early form of cheque. These were handwritten notes that enabled a customer to draw on funds in his or her account with a bank for release of payment to the specified payee. One of the earliest-known of such drawn notes in existence today dates back to 1659.

In 1717, the Bank of England pioneered the use of a pre-printed form for such payments. The form was printed on *cheque paper* to prevent fraud. Bank customers had to attend in person at the bank to obtain from the cashier a form with serial numbers on it. The written cheque received by the payee would have to be brought back to the issuing bank for settlement. This clearing process would take a number of days because of the physical cheque presentation for payment at the issuing bank.

At first, each bank sent messengers to the other banks to present cheques for collection, while keeping a tally of balances between them until they settled with each other. But this meant a lot of travelling. Then around 1770, bank messengers, getting tired of this daily routine, found a clever way of getting their job done. The banking folklore story goes that a London bank messenger stopped for a beer at the Five Bells, a tavern in Lombard Street in the City of London, and noticed another bank messenger. They got on to a conversation and realised that they each had cheques drawn on the other's bank, and decided to exchange them at the tavern and save each other the extra trip. The practice led to the birth of the cheque clearing house.

By the 1800's a dedicated space was established for the bankers' clearing house. The London clearing house used a method by which each bank paid cash to and then was paid cash by an inspector at the end of each day, similar to today's *end of day batch settlement*. This method was adopted by a number of other countries. By 1853, the New York clearing house used a large oval table and two clerks from each bank. An outer ring of clerks would rotate at set intervals, settling payments in cash with each bank in intraday batches.

It is said that in 1811 the Commercial Bank of Scotland was the first bank to personalise its customers' cheques by printing the name of the account holder vertically along the left-hand edge. Then in 1830, the Bank of England introduced cheque books of 50, 100, and 200 forms. These cheque books became a common format for the distribution of cheques to bank customers.

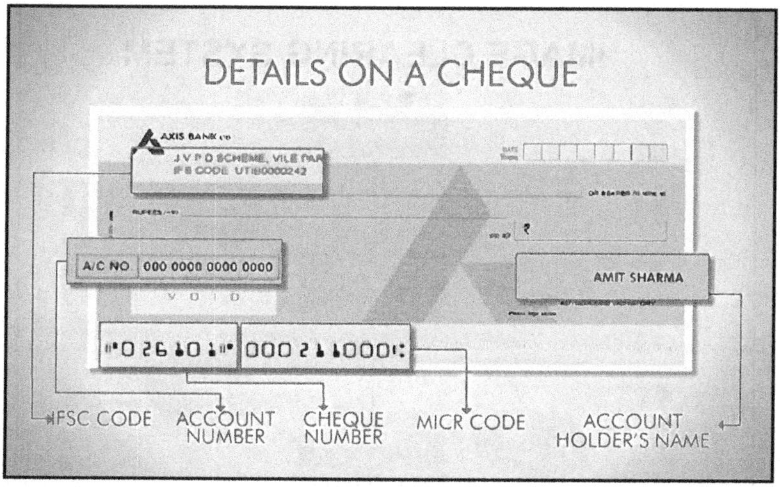

MICR characters at the bottom of a cheque; Source: Wikipedia

In 1882, the U.K. passed the Bills of Exchange Act and in 1881, India passed the Negotiable Instruments Act, both covering cheques to establish their legal status as the means of payment in the financial systems. The major acceleration in the use of cheques came in 1959 when Magnetic Ink Character Recognition (MICR) was developed. The MICR format was first developed by Stanford Research Institute and General Electric Computer Laboratory and was used for sorting cheques. This technology uses magnetically chargeable ink to print the numbers and special characters on the bottom of cheques, enabling computers to reliably read routing and account numbers and thus the sorting of paper cheques was automated.

Cheque volumes continued to grow during the 20th century and they were the most popular non-cash method for making payments with billions of them processed each year. Cheque volumes peaked in the late 1980s and early 1990s, after which electronic payment methods were pushed globally following the stock market crash of 1989.

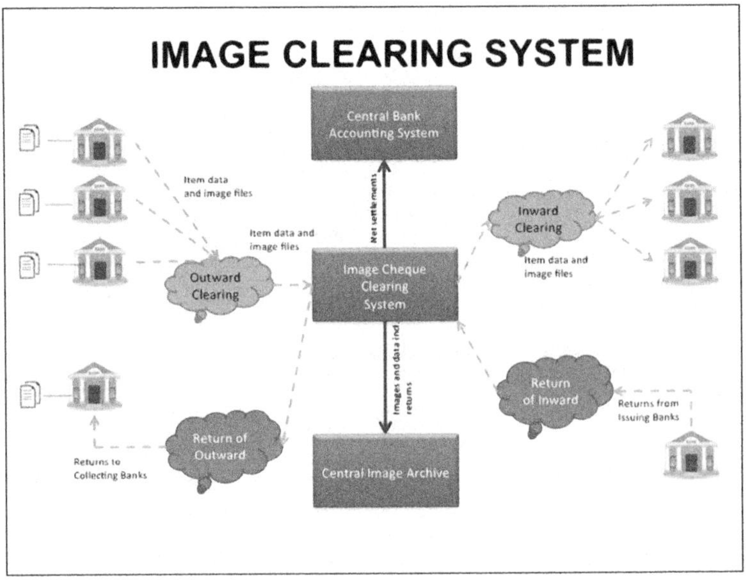

Cheque image clearing system; Source: http://www.bemoneyaware.com

From the mid-1990s, many countries enacted laws for cheque truncation allowing a physical cheque to be converted into electronic form for transmission to the paying bank or clearing house. This eliminated the process of cumbersome physical presentation and saves time and processing costs.

Cheques are still widely used in the Asia region in countries that have developed their banking systems following the British model. In Hong Kong, physical cheques were the primary means of payment, as in the rest of the world, in the 1970's and 80's. Under British rule, Hongkong and Shanghai Bank (the former name of HSBC before re-domiciling its headquarters to London) was performing many *de facto* central banking functions. In addition to issuing bank notes, it managed interbank clearing functions including a clearing house where banks would send cheques for clearing until the function was taken over by the Hong Kong Interbank Clearing Limited before 1997.

Those who were working in the financial industry in Hong Kong during the 1970's to early 90's would fondly remember a local *cha-chan-tang* (Cantonese word for café) on the slope leading to today's Lan Kwai Fong where messengers from banks and offices in Central would gather twice a day, around 10:30am in the morning and 3:30pm in the afternoon, after visiting the clearing house at Hongkong and Shanghai Bank. Nicknamed 'The Snakes Den', Cantonese slang for 'the place where messengers play truant to take a break', the café was well known for being the meeting place for messengers to exchange documents not supported by the clearing house as much as for its local style of aromatic strong coffee and tea served with carnation milk.

5. The Great Leap

Cheques were the most prevalent form of non-cash payment in the 1980's in many countries. In the U.S., the annual volume of cheques in 1983 totaled 40 billion; 90% of the population had checking accounts, and each person issued fifteen cheques per month on average.

Other developed countries such as Germany and Japan, however, were moving fast to paperless payments.

The following statistics provide interesting comparisons:

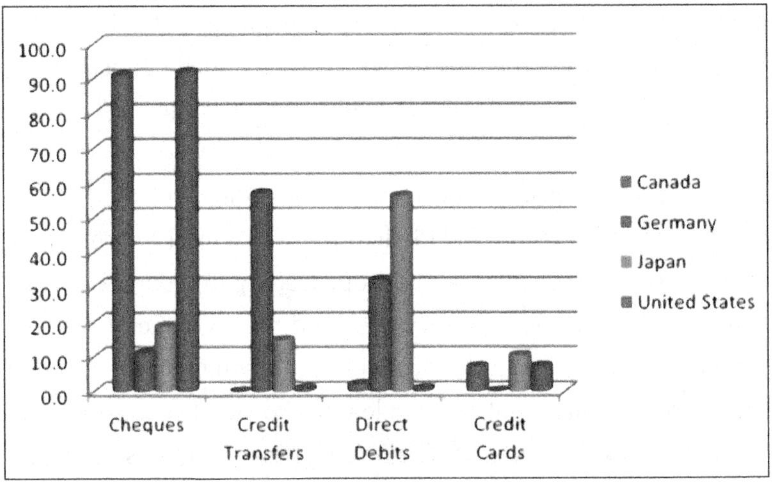

Non-cash Payment Instruments as a Percentage of Total Volume of Transactions in 1983; Source: First Chicago research data

In Asia, other than those countries under British influence, many countries were still cash-based and cheques were not widely used.

China embarked on reforming its banking system following the establishment of a formal diplomatic relationship between China and the

U.S. in December 1978. First National Bank of Chicago (First Chicago) was the first US bank approved by China to open a representative office in Beijing in 1980 after relinquishing its banking license in Taiwan. With that special status, it enjoyed very robust business growth in China during the initial years. In 1986, the People's Bank of China (PBOC), China's central bank, mandated Frist Chicago to conduct a project to make recommendations on enhancing China's payment systems. I was a member of the consulting team for the project.

In 1986, the banking industry in China was just about to launch its first phase of reform. Under the supervision of PBOC were three levels of banking institutions. The first level comprised four state-owned banks, namely: Bank of China, Industrial & Commercial Bank of China, Agricultural Bank of China, and Construction Bank of China. Each bank is structured with a well-defined hierarchy: province, county, city/town/commune. In the second level were a dozen of smaller commercial banks, and the third level hundreds and thousands of urban credit cooperatives and rural credit cooperatives.

A 'one bank' policy was enforced, such that each company could only have an account with one bank. Money transfers were very restrictive:

- All nation-wide branches were permitted to carry out inter-provincial remittances only.
- All provincial branches were permitted to carry out inter-county remittances within the province only.
- All county branches were permitted to carry out remittances within the county only.
- Cheques were available for companies only and could be used for payments within the same city only.

Money transfers could only be done in the form of either a telegraphic transfer or mail transfer. A telegraphic transfer means a cable message sent from the remitting bank to the receiving bank to effect the transfer of money. A mail transfer means a credit advice sent from the remitting bank to the receiving bank by mail requesting it to credit the transferred amount to the beneficiary's account and to debit the book of the remitting bank.

The process was paper-based and manual. When the remitting bank made a money transfer to a receiving bank located in a different province, the remitting bank would have to fill out a multi-ply credit advice. One copy would be given to the customer making the remittance, one copy would be sent to the receiving bank, and another copy would be sent to PBOC's Head Office Reconciliation Centre, where the credit advice would be input to a computer and a transaction-listing report would be produced either weekly, monthly or quarterly depending on the transaction volume of the city where the bank was located. When the receiving bank received the report from PBOC, it would manually reconcile the transactions against its own books. Discrepancies would be reported to PBOC for investigation.

The process was similar for inter-county money transfers within a province or intra-county money transfers.

Intra-city remittances, whether telegraphic transfers, mail transfers, cheques, and bank drafts were cleared through the exchange house in the city. Once or twice a day, the four banks would send messengers to the exchange house to exchange credit advices and cheques with one another manually under the supervision of PBOC.

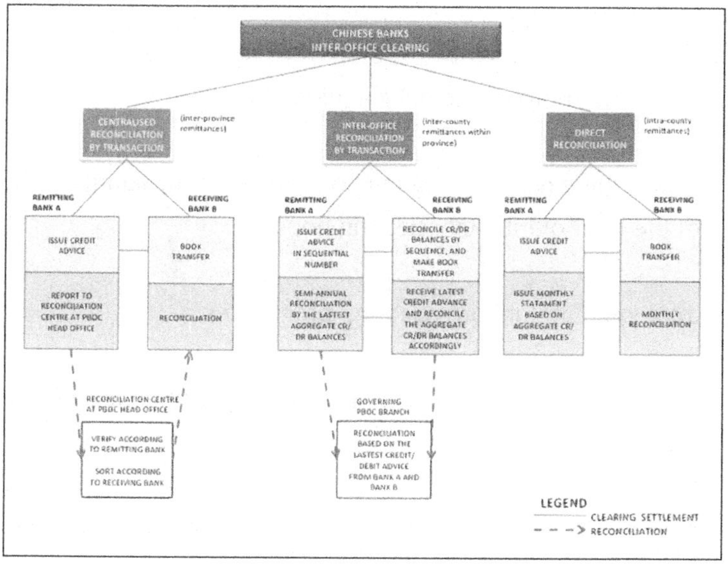

China's money transfer processing system;
Source: First Chicago consultancy report to PBOC

Due to the manual process, the clearing time was long - at least two to three days by telegraphic transfers and seven to ten days by mail transfers. The lost float had very significant negative impact on liquidity in the banking system.

How to shorten settlement and fund-availability time was the objective of our project commissioned by PBOC.

China's GDP per capita in 1985 was only US$249 according to World Bank's data, compared with US$10,787 in Japan and US$17,134 in the U.S. We had to come up with short-term and long-term improvement recommendations within the constraints of limited telecommunication infrastructure and a limited expenditure budget for computerisation.

It was an interesting challenge. We made several field trips to China and completed the project in four months.

For short-term improvements, we recommended quick fixes by strengthening the paper-based system to reduce clearing time for quick wins to improve interbank liquidity by:

- establishing regional clearing houses across the country on top of the layer of intra-city clearing houses.

- implementing uniform clearing procedures.

- introducing a unique numbering system for cheques and payment orders.

- processing cheques at PBOC twenty-four hours a day running three shifts.

- developing a courier system for moving cheques and money orders to regional clearing centres including:

  * ground transportation (motor vehicles, bicycles) in suburban and rural areas.

  * air transportation between major cities.

For long-term improvements, we recommended the development of alternative payment systems quickly to leverage on new technology to bypass the paper-based system by:

- establishing a nation-wide electronic clearing system managed by PBOC.

- developing an electronic Fed wire type system for immediate availability of funds.

The recommendations were presented to and discussed with various PBOC teams in a full day seminar, followed by a celebration dinner at the Summer Palace hosted by a PBOC Vice Governor. While the feedback was very positive, we did not know to what extent our recommendations were being implemented. Disappointingly, PBOC did not engage us further in consulting for upgrading or expanding the payment systems after the project.

Meanwhile, First Chicago also became history after the merger with Bank One in 1998 to form Bank One Corporation, which in turn was merged with Chase in 2004.

What we learnt in public news was that PBOC started to develop a national interbank system based on satellite communication networks in 1991 to speed up interbank payments across regions. It also organised and built up intra-province and intra-city local clearings systems to shorten the clearing process for local remittances and money transfers in order to reduce the float and improve liquidity. The state-owned banks also established advanced electronic exchange systems.

Thirty years onwards, China's GDP per capita has grown over 3,000% to US$7,594 in 2014. It has leap-frogged the cheque system altogether in its payment infrastructure development, which was the right decision as recommended in the First Chicago study. It has now become a leading country in electronic payments especially Internet-based e-commerce payments along with transformation in the society's online purchasing behaviours using mobile devices.

In Q1 2016, China racked up US$387 billion in online retail sales - the world's largest market for e-commerce.

We estimate the number of online shoppers will exceed 660 million by 2023..., commented a Morgan Stanley analyst.[3]

China's digital and e-commerce revolution has begun.

3 *China's e-Commerce Revolution*, 13 March 2015, *Morgan Stanley Blue Papers.*

6. The Nine Commandments

At the time when securities clearing and settlement were paper-based, the process involved brokers and dealers using either messengers or the mail to send certificates and cheques to settle the trades, which posed a huge risk and incurred high transaction costs.

In the late 1960's, The New York Stock Exchange experienced an unprecedented surge in trading with volumes shooting up to nearly fifteen million shares a day in April 1968, as opposed to five million a day just three years earlier - which at the time had already been considered overwhelming. The paperwork burden became enormous. Stock certificates were left for weeks piled haphazardly on any level surface, including filing cabinets and tables. Stocks were mailed to wrong addresses or not mailed at all. Overtime and night work became mandatory. Staff turnover was 60% a year.

To resolve the crisis, two initiatives were implemented:

The first was to hold the certificates at a central depository (sometimes referred to as '*certificate immobilisation*') and record change of ownership with a *book-entry accounting system* that was eventually done electronically. This led the New York Stock Exchange to establish the Central Certificate Service (CCS) in 1968 and finally the development of Depository Trust Company (DTC) in 1973.

The second involved the implementation of *multilateral netting* to further reduce the number of transactions. Brokers had accounts at central depository, the DTC, which acted as Counter-party to every trade. So instead of sending payments and securities for each transaction, trades and payments were simply aggregated over the course of the day for each member broker and then were settled at the end of the day by transferring the net difference in securities and funds from one account at the depository to another.

These measures marked the first major evolution of the clearing and settlement process. But the ultimate transformation occurred as a response to the Black Monday market crash of October 1987.

In late 1985 and early 1986, the US economy began a rapidly growing recovery from the recessions of the early 1980's. The stock market advanced significantly, with the Dow peaking in August 1987 at 2,722 points.

In the U.K., the Margaret Thatcher government launched a programme of privatisation of nationalised industries in the 1980's. The Big Bang of 1986 led to an explosion in the volume of trades.

Time magazine cover: The Stock Market Crash 1987; Source: Wikipedia

On 19 October 1987, commonly known as the *Black Monday*, stock markets around the world crashed and shredded a huge value within a very short time. The crash began in Hong Kong and spread west to Europe, hitting the United States after other markets had already declined by a significant margin. The Dow Jones Industrial Average fell 22.61% from 508 points to 1,738.74. The S&P 500 dropped 20.4%, falling from 282.7 points to 225.06. This was the greatest loss Wall Street had ever suffered on a single day.

The sharp crash in stock prices during *Black Monday* placed extreme stress on financial clearing and settlement. Many investors sought to limit their losses by selling their securities, but were not able to do so and found that the failure of timely settlement left them exposed.

Hong Kong was especially impacted. Ronald Li Fook-Shiu was the Chairman of the Hong Kong Stock Exchange at the time. He came from a prominent family in the city's business, political and judicial circles.[4] Born on the first day of Chinese Lunar New Year in 1929, the same year that the stock market crashed in New York triggering the US Great Depression, he was the youngest son of the twelve children of Li Koon-Chun. He was brilliant in the markets, dabbling in stocks from the age of six. He made history in 1969 by founding the Far East Stock Exchange with his brother, Li Fook-Hing, to break the Hong Kong Club's monopoly in the buying and selling of stocks, later being called Godfather of the Stock Market. In 1986, he helped merge the Far East Stock Exchange with three other exchanges into the Hong Kong Stock Exchange - precursor of today's Hong Kong

---

4 *The Li family was one of the city's four most prominent families at the time. His brother, Simon Li Fook-Sean, was the first Chinese judge to serve as chief justice and also ran for chief executive ahead of the handover. Among his other nephews are Bank of East Asia chairman David Li Kwok-Po, former education minister and now Executive Council member Professor Arthur Li Kwok-Cheung, and Academy of Medicine president Dr. Donald Li Kwok-Tung. Source: Finance sector says farewell to its 'headmaster' Ronald Li Fook-Shiu, 31 December, 2114, South China Morning Post.*

Exchanges and Clearing - creating one of the world's largest and most dynamic bourse operators worth US$26 million in market cap. He became its first chairman.

During the Black Monday crash, he decided to close the doors of the stock market for four days to shield it from the storm battering the rest of the world. All investors, local and international, were caught by the unexpected gating decision. It drew immense criticism. At the press conference announcing the decision, one of the lasting images was of Ronald Li pounding on the table in anger in full view of television cameras, threatening to sue a reporter who questioned the legality of the closing of the exchange. When the market reopened, the Hang Seng Index tumbled by 33%. As a result, the Hong Kong stock market earned the sobriquet of being a Mickey Mouse market by some commentators.

Godfather of Hong Kong stock market: Ronald Li; Source: we.ejinsight.com

Ronald Li later had a dramatic fall from grace. He was arrested by the Independent Commission Against Corruption (ICAC) in December 1987 and was convicted in 1991 of taking bribes in return for approving listings during his office as the Chairman of the Hong

Kong Stock Exchange in 1987. He was sent to Stanley Prison and served thirty months of a four-year sentence.

He was reportedly worth HK$10 billion at the time of his imprisonment. His stock portfolio was said to have earned nearly HK$5 million a day during his incarceration. He died in 2014 after battling cancer for several years, aged eighty-seven.

Recognising the dangers of severe price swings to global clearing, thirty large international banks calling themselves *The Group of Thirty (G30)* came together under the leadership of John Reed, then Chairman of Citibank, and issued the report '*Clearance and Settlement Systems in the World's Securities Markets*' with nine recommendations for reducing risk in cross-border securities settlement.

The G30 recommendations of 1989 provided the general principles for ensuring an efficient and low-risk clearing settlement environment, including: shortening settlement time, setting up of book-entry settlement procedures and a central depository, adopting delivery against payment rules, netting trades while using same-day-funds, accepting *International Standards Organisation* (ISO) guidelines for security identification and messages, and promoting the lending and borrowing of securities to ease settlement.

The G30 recommendations altered the priorities of securities markets around the world dramatically. Settlement issues were brought out from back offices into the limelight and became the topic of many discussions.

One of the recommendations was for all markets to adopt '*Trade Date plus three Rolling Settlement*' to shorten settlement time and reduce market risk.

In implementing this recommendation, Hong Kong was put into a unique position. Hong Kong had been adopting a twenty-four-hour settlement rule during the 1980's. The share settlement system required physical delivery between brokers, involving massive movements of paper and cumbersome procedures. An additional complication was that, after settlement, if investors wanted immediately to exercise the rights attached to the shares, the re-registration process took up to twenty-one days before new shares were available. As a result, most shares were held in street names outside of books-close periods. They thus became, in effect, bearer shares, with registration highly concentrated immediately prior to the record date for dividends or rights. The system lacked security and was prone to creating high pressure on the settlement process during times of high market activity.

The unification of the four stock exchanges, together with the introduction of computer-assisted dealing in 1986, resulted in a substantial increase in both trading volumes and in the level of international participation. During the bull market of 1986-87, it became very difficult for all trades to comply with the twenty-four-hour rule, even for transactions in which all the participants were local.

While the need to lengthen the settlement period was accepted, it was not an easy decision. The Stock Exchange's statistics showed that about 75% of trades were settled consistently on T+1, i.e. within the rule. Thus, the majority of brokers and investors were operating comfortably on T+1. To extend the settlement period to T+2 would be considered as a step backward in the sense that it penalised the efficient majority of brokers to accept a doubling of the settlement period and consequently greater market risk.

But to maintain Hong Kong's position as an open and international economy, the reputation of which had been undermined by the four-day stock market closure, the Stock Exchange members had to take fully into account the needs of international investors and the impact of time zones on their settlement. Take for instance a settlement case involving a fund manager in Sydney, an underlying beneficiary in New York, a global custodian in London and a sub-custodian in Hong Kong. The settlement would require T+2 to complete, not twenty-four hours.

After lengthy and spirited debates, members of the Hong Kong Stock Exchange agreed to shift from T+1 to T+2 even though the G30 recommendation was to implement T+3.

Agreement was reached to get in place a central clearing and settlement system by the end of 1991 that would enable centralised broker-to-broker net settlement and book-entry delivery and transfer of uncertificated shareholdings. Trading data would be transferred by the Stock Exchange to the Hong Kong Securities Clearing Company (HKSCC) for processing after close of the market on trade day. Electronic links would connect up all participants. Money transfers would be through the established banking system. HKSCC would guarantee all trades in Hong Kong stocks on the Stock Exchange locked into the system at the time of trade-data transfer.

Whilst other exchanges around the world were attempting to compress their existing settlement periods to T+3, Hong Kong rationalised its settlement rules by extending its settlement period to T+2, running ahead of its peers around the world.

The G30 recommendations were upheld by the industry as The Nine Commandments for benchmarking the risk elements of each market.

As to the tenth commandment, which was not written in the G30 report, there were various unofficial versions, from the biblical Thou shall not covet, to the consoling May the best man win, to the philosophical Let the invisible hand rule...

Appendix: G30 Recommendations 1989

1: Trade Comparison on Trade Date plus 1

By 1990, all comparisons of trade between direct market participants (i.e. brokers, dealers and other exchange members) should be accomplished by T+1.

2: Trade Comparison for Indirect Participants

Indirect market participants (such as institutional investors, or any trading counterparties which are not broker/dealers) should, by 1992, be members of a trade comparison system which achieves positive affirmation of trade details.

3: Central Depository

Each country should have an effective and fully developed central securities depository, organised and managed to encourage the broadest possible industry participation (directly or indirectly), in place by 1992.

4: Netting

Each country should study its market and participation to determine whether a trade netting system would be beneficial in terms of reducing risk and promoting efficiency. If a netting system would be appropriate, it should be implemented by 1992.

5: Delivery Versus Payment

Delivery versus payment (DVP) should be employed as the method for settling all securities transactions. A DVP system should be in place by 1992.

6: Same-Day Funds

Payments associated with the settlement of securities transactions and the servicing of securities portfolios should be made consistent across all instruments and markets by adopting the 'same day' funds convention.

7: Trade Date plus three Rolling Settlement

A rolling settlement system should be adopted by all markets. Final settlement should occur on Trade Date plus three by 1992.

8: Securities Lending

Securities lending and borrowing should be encouraged as a method of expediting the settlement of securities transactions. Existing regulatory and taxation barriers that inhibit the practice of lending securities should be removed.

9: Use of ISO Standards 7775 and 6166

Each country should adopt the standard for securities messages developed by the International Organisation for Standardisation (ISO 7775). In particular, countries should adopt the SIN numbering system for securities issues as defined in the ISO standard 6166, at least for the cross-border transaction.

Source: www.group30.org

7. Risk Controllers

In January 2003, *The Group of Thirty (G30)* published another report entitled '*Global Clearing and Settlement: A Plan of Action*'. The *Global Clearing and Settlement Project*, led by Sir Andrew Large, Deputy Governor of Bank of England, identified areas where progress was being made as well as where little or no progress was apparent since the previous report published in 1989.

The 2003 report recommended wide-ranging reform of the clearing and settlement process, including creation and implementation of global standards in technological and operational areas, improvements in risk-management practices, further harmonisation of global legal and regulatory environments, and improved governance for providers of clearing and settlement services. These changes were embodied in twenty recommendations aimed at significantly improving the safety and efficiency of international securities markets.

One of the recommendations was to '*expand the use of central counter-parties*'. This was a step further than in the G30 recommendation of 1989 to establish central depository in each country.

A Central Counter-party (CCP) performs two *clearing* functions:

- Once a transaction has been agreed between two parties and registered with a CCP, the CCP inserts itself into the transaction (so that one contract becomes two - a process called *netting by novation*) and is deemed to become the buyer to every seller and the seller to every buyer.

- Then instead of sending payments and securities for each transaction, the CCP will net transactions between members

> on a multilateral basis, which means that a delivery of a security due to the CCP from parties A and B can be netted off against deliveries of the same security due on the same day from the CCP to parties C and D. The same applies to cash payments. This produces much smaller net exposures than bilateral netting, in which each party can only net transactions with the same counter-party.

For example, if a broker bought 100 shares of Apple for a customer and sold 50 shares of Apple for another customer, then the broker's net position is the accumulation of 50 shares of Apple, which would be recorded at the end of the market day. If the broker paid US$100 per share to buy the 100 shares of Apple stock and sold the 50 shares for the same price on the same day, then the net difference plus transaction costs is debited from the broker's account at the end of the market day, and credited to the account of the CCP. Likewise, only 50 shares of Apple would be transferred to the broker's account, since this is the net difference of buying 100 shares and selling 50 shares.

CCPs benefit both parties in a transaction because they bear most of the credit risk. If two individuals deal with one another, the buyer bears the credit risk of the seller, and vice versa. When a CCP is used, the credit risk that is held against both buyer and seller is coming from the CCP, which in all likelihood is much less than in the bilateral situation.

CCPs are interesting creations, arising through gradual and experimental evolution from clearing houses. Clearing houses have been organised since the 1800's for banks to net cheques and other transactions. In the 19th century, they started supporting their members in times of bank crisis and panics by offering three forms of support:

- Firstly, all members jointly suspended withdrawal of deposits.
- Secondly, the clearing house ceased publication of bank members' individual financial information to the public so that they would not know which banks were strong and which ones had financial difficulties.
- Thirdly, the clearing house issued money called 'clearing house loan certificates' to the public in small denominations.

The loan certificates were effectively money that was a joint obligation of all bank members. Instead of depositors withdrawing their cash from a bank member, they accepted certificates that were treated like money and were a joint obligation of all clearing house members. That way, the clearing house association effectively became the 'lender of last resort' to its member banks by mutualising the risks among all members.

Clearing House Loan Certificates are seen as the most important development in US banking during the 19th century. They created liquidity during times of crisis, which occurred regularly during that era. They prevented banks that did not have financial problems from forced liquidation. For example, during the panic of 1893, US$100 million of Clearing House Loan Certificates were issued nationally. During the panic of 1907, a total of US$500 million Loan Certificates was issued nationally. These still seem like large numbers now, so consider the relative size over a hundred years ago. To put it in perspective, in 1907 that was US$500 million that would have been withdrawn from the banking system, but was not, due to the success and support of the clearing house. Not surprisingly, the clearing house was the model and framework for the Federal Reserve when it was created in 1913.

There is no clear conclusion as to which was the earliest CCP in the world. The history of Chicago Board of Trade (CBOT) is an interesting example illustrating the evolution from a clearing house to a CCP. Very early on, the CBOT recognised the importance of creating incentives for adherence to its rules, including the contractual obligations of counter-parties to contracts traded on the exchange. Initially, the primary incentive was the penalty that a member that defaulted on its obligations could be barred from the trading floor. This consequence was no doubt a powerful incentive for solvent members to meet their obligations, but an insolvent member might not put significant value to the loss of trading privileges in adverse financial situations.

By 1873, the CBOT recognised the importance of evaluating the solvency of its members and adopted a resolution stipulating that any member whose solvency was questioned must open its financial accounts to inspection and could be expelled if it refused to do so. Around the same time, the exchange introduced initial and variation margin requirements for contracts traded on the exchange and set strict time limits for the posting of margin deposits. Failure to post margin deposits would be considered a default on the member's contracts.

In 1925, the CBOT formed the Board of Trade Clearing Corporation (BOTCC), a true CCP that became the Counter-party to all transactions on the exchange. With the creation of BOTCC, members of the exchange were required to purchase shares in the clearing house, and only the member shareholders were permitted to use the facility. Members were also required to post their margin deposits with the clearing house. In the event of a member's default, the clearing house would take responsibility for settling the defaulting member's trades. The clearing house would seek to cover any losses incurred in settling the defaulter's obligations by liquidating its margin deposit. But if the losses exceeded the value of the margin, the deficiency would be charged against the clearing house's capital, including the capital owned by the non-defaulting members. If the losses were so severe as to deplete the clearing house's capital, the members could be required to purchase additional shares.

Chicago Board of Trade Building in Chicago, Illinois; Source: Wikipedia

This organisational arrangement to mutualise risk has been adopted by many other CCPs, both for exchange-traded derivatives and for cash securities transactions. It creates incentives for all the exchange's members to support the imposition of risk controls that limit the extent to which the trading activities of any individual member expose all other members to losses from defaults. Moreover, because the members own the clearing house, they have the capability to act on their incentives for effective CCP risk management.

These arrangements illustrate how market forces can produce private regulations that address concerns about safety, soundness, and broader financial stability.

Since the G30 report in 2003, the use of a CCP has become most prevalent in clearing activities. CCPs are commonly organised as separate legal entities from the securities depositories even though the CCP can be closely related to a CSD, but each has a distinct role and responsibilities in the clearing and settlement process.

In Asia, the implementation of CCPs has expanded from stock markets to the bond markets including emerging markets like China, Indonesia, Malaysia and Thailand.

During the global financial crisis in 2008 following the collapse of Lehman Brothers, CCPs successfully completed trades worth trillions of Dollars for a multitude of financial instruments across listed and over-the-counter markets.

Dubbed as the 'Risk Controllers',[5] CCPs have helped avert a global financial Armageddon.

5 *The Risk Controllers: Central Counter-party Clearing in Globalised Financial Markets*, Peter Norman, published by John Wiley & Son in December 2007.

Appendix: G30 Recommendations 2003

CREATING A STRENGTHENED, INTEROPERABLE GLOBAL NETWORK

1. Eliminate paper and automate communication, data capture, and enrichment.

2. Harmonise messaging standards and communication protocols.

3. Develop and implement reference data standards.

4. Synchronise timing between different clearing and settlement systems and associated payment and foreign-exchange systems.

5. Automate and standardise institutional trade matching.

6. Expand the use of central counter-parties.

7. Permit securities lending and borrowing to expedite settlement.

8. Automate and standardise asset servicing processes, including corporate actions, tax relief arrangements, and restrictions on foreign ownership.

MITIGATING RISK

9. Ensure the financial integrity of providers of clearing and settlement services.

10. Reinforce the risk-management practices of users of clearing and settlement service providers.

11. Ensure final, simultaneous transfer and availability of assets.

12. Ensure effective business-continuity and disaster-recovery planning.

13. Address the possibility of failure of a systemically important institution.

14. Strengthen assessment of the enforceability of contracts.

15. Advance legal certainty over rights to securities, cash, or collateral.

16. Recognise and support improved valuation methodologies and closeout netting arrangements.

IMPROVING GOVERNANCE

17. Ensure appointment of appropriately experienced and senior board members.

18. Promote fair access to securities clearing and settlement networks.

19. Ensure equitable and effective attention to stakeholder interests.

20. Encourage consistent regulation and oversight of securities clearing and settlement service providers.

Source: www.group30.org

8. Something Never Changes

Greed, for lack of a better word, is good... declared Gekko, played by Michael Douglas, in the Hollywood film *Wall Street* in 1987.

Greed, despite the role it plays in many financial innovations, has been the primary driver for many market abnormalities.

Market bubbles and crashes are far from being modern-day social economic phenomenon. Long before speculators piled their bets on stocks, bonds, currencies, gold, silver or crude oil and created market bubbles, the first market mania happened in 1600's with speculations on a beautiful flower - the tulip.

The tulip was first introduced to Holland around 1593. It has a saturated, intense petal color that no other plant exhibits. With its ability to tolerate the harsh weather conditions in Holland, the flower grew quickly in popularity.

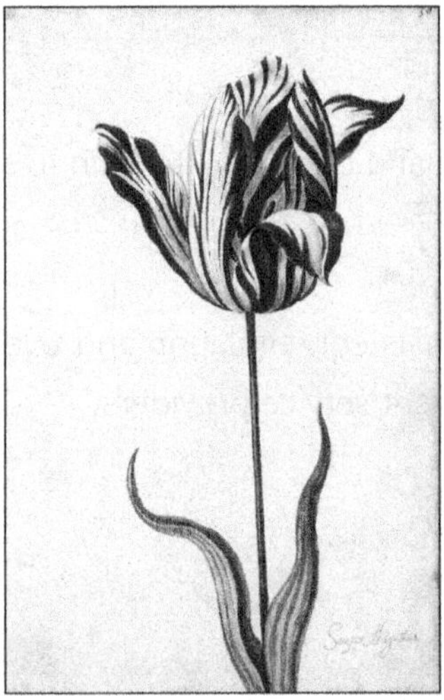

Image of a tulip plant; Source: Wikipedia

Tulips bloom in April and May for only about a week. During the plant's dormant phase from June to September, bulbs can be uprooted for buying and selling. During the rest of the year, florists or tulip traders negotiated and signed contracts before a notary to purchase tulips at the end of the season *(futures contracts)*. This created a market for tulip bulb futures, and many of the techniques of modern finance have developed from this.

At first, tulips were sold at standardised prices. As the flowers grew in popularity, professional growers paid higher and higher prices for bulbs, and prices rose steadily. By 1634, in part as a result of demand from the French, speculators began to enter the market and prices rapidly increased year after year.

Soon, any tulip bulb could fetch hundreds of Guilders. In 1636, the Dutch created a type of formal futures market where contracts to buy bulbs at the end of the season were bought and sold. Even everyday people got involved as a means to supplement their incomes or dream of a quick rise to wealth.

Tulip mania reached its peak during the winter of 1636-37, when some bulbs were reportedly changing hands ten times in a day. No deliveries were ever made to fulfil any of these contracts because, in February 1637, tulip-bulb contract prices collapsed abruptly and the trade in tulips ground to a halt.

The collapse began in Haarlem when, for the first time, buyers apparently refused to show up at a routine bulb auction. Only sellers existed and there were no buyers at all. Haarlem was then at the height of an outbreak of bubonic plague, so this may have been the reason why. Nonetheless, within days, panic had spread across the country. Despite the efforts of traders to prop up demand, the market for tulips evaporated. Flowers that had commanded 5,000 Guilders a few weeks before now fetched one-hundredth that amount.

Greed and irrationality pushes up the value of an item in disproportion to its real value, and the crowd behaviour to speculate and profit overtakes its sense of logic.

It is said that Joe Kennedy, a famous rich guy in his day and an avid investor, exited the stock market in timely fashion in the winter of 1928 after he started to hear stock tips from his shoe-shine boy.

The Life and Times of Joseph P. Kennedy by William J. Duncliffe describes his progress:

.... his intuitive sense told him that the mad stock market spree could not possibly last; that, like a roller coaster, it would ultimately have to come back to earth. Kennedy found himself having to elbow his way into brokers' offices, past the jostling crowds of eager-eyed overnight experts who were shouting orders to buy, buy, and buy again—on margin.

One day he found himself stopping at a shoe-shine parlour on Wall Street.

'The kid who shined my shoes didn't know me, he said. He wasn't looking for a tip on the market or anything like that. He was just average and, like everyone else, he was playing the market. All the time he was snapping the polishing cloth over my shoes, he kept telling me what was going to happen that day, what stocks would rise and what the market would do.

I just listened to him, and when I left the place I thought, "When the time comes that a shoe-shine boy knows as much as I do about what is going on in the stock market, tells me so, and is entirely correct, there's something wrong with either me or the market, and it's time for me to get out".'

Bernard Baruch, another investor, echoed his theory and described the scene before the Crash as follows:

'Taxi drivers told you what to buy. The shoe-shine boy could give you a summary of the day's financial news as he worked with rag and polish. An old beggar who regularly patrolled the street in front of my office now gave me tips and, I suppose, spent the money I and others gave him in the market. My cook had a brokerage account and followed the ticker closely. Her paper profits were quickly blown away in the gale of 1929.'

The shoe-shine boy was buying because the market was going up and he saw it as an opportunity to get rich and stop shining the shoes of Joe Kennedy and Bernard Baruch. He was buying not because he believed the economy would perform well in the future nor because he had some deep understanding of the fundamentals of the companies whose stocks he was buying; he was buying because everyone else was doing it and getting rich and he wanted to claim his piece of the profits.

Less than a year later, stock markets around the world collapsed, leaving tens of millions of people impoverished for decades to come.

These same scenes of the early 1900's have replayed in many Asian countries during market booms and busts. Those working in Central during the 1980's and 1990's would remember the long row of shoe-shine men (child labour had been made illegal in Hong Kong) along Theatre Lane in Central. During market bull runs in those days, one would hear exactly the same conversations between the shoe-shine men with their customers in pin-striped suits.

Theatre Lane today; Source: Wikipedia

Marc Faber, the investment analyst based in Hong Kong best known for his persistent pessimism, had an even more provocative version of this market behaviour theory.

He argued in his publication *The Great Money Illusion* in 1995 that attending nightclubs could help predict the stock market: 'If nightclub hostesses start offering advice on shares, it's time to sell'.

Club Bboss during its heyday in the 1980s; Source: Wikipedia

Fast-forward twenty years to the summer of 2015, the China stock market saw the worst bubble burst in history.

Tyler Durden in his commentary in zerohedge.com on 24 June 2015 remarked: 'When your banana guy starts trading stocks, you know it's over....'

The photo below says it all:

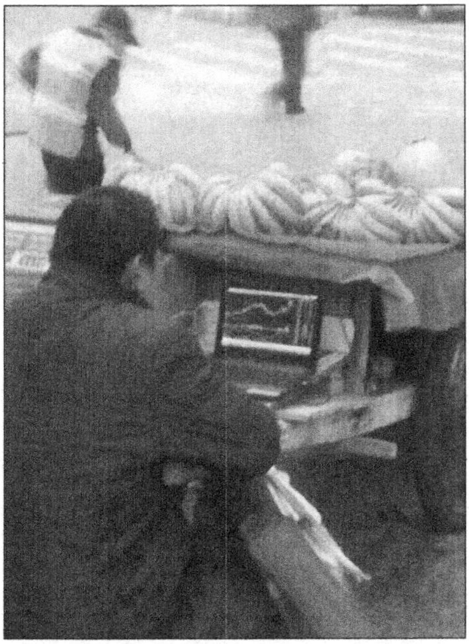

Everyone is a stock trader: street hawker monitoring stock market movements; Source: @wmiddlekoop

Market behaviour never changes.

9. Collapse of Barings

Harry's Bar has been opening its doors at the busy historic riverfront commercial stretch of Boat Quay adjacent to Raffles Place in Singapore for over twenty years. It is featured in *Lonely Planet* and practically every tourist guidebook as one of the best bars in Singapore, boasting of its jazz music and classic American cuisine from steak to burgers. On its drink menu is a house cocktail named the Bank Breaker, which pays homage to the dubious Nick Leeson who used to hang out in the bar with other traders after work during Asia's economic boom in the early 1990's. A mixture of Midori, whisky and a double measure of soda water, it is sweet and goes down smoothly but, aptly, has a deceptive kick that takes you by surprise.

In 1995, it shocked the financial world globally when Barings - one of the oldest investment banks in the U.K. - collapsed as a result of massive losses created due to unauthorised trading by its head derivatives trader in the Singapore office, Nick Leeson.

The Harry's Bar at Boat Quay; Source: Openrice.com

Harry's general manager at that time, Margaret Woodward, said of the bankers and traders who frequented the bar: 'Nick was always with a group of guys who were big rollers, big spenders. They all were in those days.... But they were nice guys, never any trouble, just boisterous'.[6]

She said she saw Leeson's fellow traders tear up Singapore hundred-Dollar bills and burn them for kicks.

The mid-nineties were heady days for traders in Singapore. Traders were young and greed was good. They had been operating in a bull market for a decade and everyone had been raking in a fortune. And then the house of cards started coming down.

Nick Leeson was from a working class family during the Thatcher revolution in the U.K. His father, Harry, was a workaday plasterer and raised his family in a public housing project in Watford, north of London. Nick never went to college. After graduating from high school, he started as a clerk in one of the stuffiest private banks, in the Coutts & Co, in 1985 at the age of eighteen. Then he accepted a role in the futures and options division at Morgan Stanley International in June 1987. Aged twenty, he was earning £20,000 a year. But he quit to join Barings in July 1989 and worked in the London settlements division for futures and options for nine months. He craved working in the fast-paced tiger economies and was transferred to Jakarta, the Indonesian capital, where he dealt with unclaimed share certificates. In March 1992, following Barings' acquisition of a seat on the Singapore International Monetary Exchange (SIMEX), he was transferred to Singapore.

Leeson arrived in Singapore in April 1992 as a derivatives operations manager of Barings Futures Singapore (BFS). He became a trader

6 *Leeson Faces 'Bank Breaker' Legacy*, 1 July 1999, *The Moscow Times.*

after passing the Institute of Banking and Finance's Futures Trading Test in June 1992. When BFS started trading on the SIMEX in July 1992, Leeson was of one of two traders at that time.

He was trading a rather simple index arbitrage strategy. The contracts he bought and sold - futures on the Nikkei 225 - were traded both in Singapore and in Osaka. In theory, there should not have been much of a price discrepancy between the two markets, but in practice there was. He watched for those arbitrage openings and traded to profit from differences in the prices. It was easy money.

Soon, instead of buying on one market and immediately selling on another market for a small profit, he was approved by his superiors to buy on one market and then held on to the contract, gambling on the future direction of the Japanese markets.

Under BFS's management structure, Leeson was not only floor manager for Barings' trading on the SIMEX but also its head of settlement operations. In the latter role, he was charged with ensuring accurate accounting for the unit. These positions would normally have been held by two different employees. By allowing him, as trading floor manager, to settle his own trades, Barings short-circuited normal accounting and internal control and audit safeguards. In effect, Leeson was able to operate with no supervision from London, an arrangement that made it easy for him to hide his losses.

In July 1992, Leeson was instructed to open an error account, the 88888 account, for BFS to report errors made by inexperienced staff of BFS. However, he used the account for his own unauthorised trading.

In an interview years later, Leeson reflected: 'While I was on the trading floor, I lost one day. I did report it to the people in Tokyo who asked me to pass it to London. I didn't do that and it went into the now infamous five eight (88888) account.... I expected to get caught on day one. I had worked in settlements myself and knew that the first thing you do every morning was a position check and that would have exposed the error'.[7]

Because of the absence of oversight, Leeson was able to make seemingly small gambles in the futures arbitrage market at BFS and covered his shortfalls by altering the records. Any profitable trades were booked to Tokyo, and any loses went into the 88888 account. He started to take more and more risk to get the losses back and aggressively traded in futures and options on the SIMEX. The losses started to mount.

The first audit was three months after the losses started. 'I didn't have any idea how to hide the loss. There was no pre-thought to any of this. So I asked London for US$5 million over the year-end and reflected it as paying off the 88888 account. None of this is rocket science, and I hope you can see there was a serious lack of common sense throughout the whole episode......I ran a loss of up to US$20 million towards the end of that year. In May of 1993, I managed to get it back in credit......During all of this period, there were visits from auditors and regulators, internal and external. Many of whom saw activity on the 88888 account but did nothing about it.'

The Singapore office was a relatively small operation, but Barings Futures surprised London with the money it made in 1993 that accounted for 20% of the firm's overall profit. And Leeson took advantage.

'I was selling at-the-money options and straddles. I'm often asked why, and if there was a strategy. The answer is no. I just needed money, and lots of it, to hide the losses. What I was doing was postponing

7 *The Jamaica Observer*, International Edition, Nov. 30, 2004

the realisation of the losses on a month-by-month basis. I did that by selling the options. As one month's options expired, I would sell the next available month's option.

The markets started falling, my losses started increasing, and, as a result, my position was increasing dynamically with it.... The movie (*Rogue Trader*) depicts an episode where I'm looking in the mirror and coming to terms with the fact that I lost US$50 million in one day. Believe me, that was one of the better days.'

By December 1994, Leeson had lost Barings £200 million; he reported to the British tax authorities a £102 million profit.

His luck ran out when the Kobe earthquake struck on 17 January 1995 and the Nikkei wobbled. Leeson bet on a rapid recovery by the Nikkei. Worried that the market would fall below 18,500, he bought Nikkei futures on a huge scale in an attempt to push it up. On 23 January, the Nikkei plunged 1,000 points to under 17,800 - 5.6% of its value on that day. Leeson was desperate and made desperate attempts to buy more Nikkei futures to force the market up. By mid-February 1995, he had accumulated an enormous position—half of the open interest in the Nikkei future and 85% of the open interest in the JGB future. The market was aware of this and probably traded against him. The position that he had in the 88888 account had just got too large, and there was no way he could get out of it.

On 23 February 1995, Leeson left Singapore to fly to Kuala Lumpur. Barings Bank auditors finally discovered the fraud around the same time that Barings' chairman, Peter Baring, received a confession note from Leeson. Leeson's activities had generated losses totaling £827 million (US$1.3 billion), twice the bank's available trading capital. The collapse cost another £100 million.

The Bank of England attempted an unsuccessful weekend bail-out. Barings was declared insolvent on 26 February 1995, and appointed administrators began managing the finances of Barings Group and its subsidiaries.

On 2 March 1995, Leeson was arrested at Frankfurt airport on his way to sneak back to the U.K. A few days after Nick Leeson's arrest in Frankfurt, Barings Bank was sold to Dutch banking and insurance giant ING for the paltry sum of £1, bringing to an end more than 230 years of banking history. In May, ING purged twenty-one Barings senior executives who were implicated in the failure to control Leeson and connected with its collapse.

Leeson was extradited to Singapore for trial on 23 November. He pleaded guilty to two charges of forgery and cheating and was sentenced in December to six-and-a-half years in prison in Singapore. During his detention, he was diagnosed for colon cancer and had surgery, but managed to recover. His marriage broke down and his wife, Lisa, remarried.

In prison, Leeson wrote an autobiography *Rogue Trader* in which he detailed his actions leading to the collapse of Barings. The book was published in 1996 and Leeson reportedly received a US$700,000 advance to pay for his huge legal bills. The book was later made into a film starring Ewan McGregor as Leeson and Anna Friel as Lisa, and Leeson received a 5% cut of the profits.

In the book, he condemned the lack of oversight that allowed him to gamble with such large amounts of money unchecked: 'The regulatory authorities were poor. On a daily basis, I could represent between 60 per cent and 80 per cent of the daily volume on SIMEX and at least 40 per cent of the open interest. These levels of trading should have attracted more of the exchange's attention. If anything, they attracted less. There was a SIMEX awards ceremony in 1994 when the management came out to receive the award for the top customer for volume on SIMEX. The 88888 accounts probably represented 95 per cent of that customer volume...

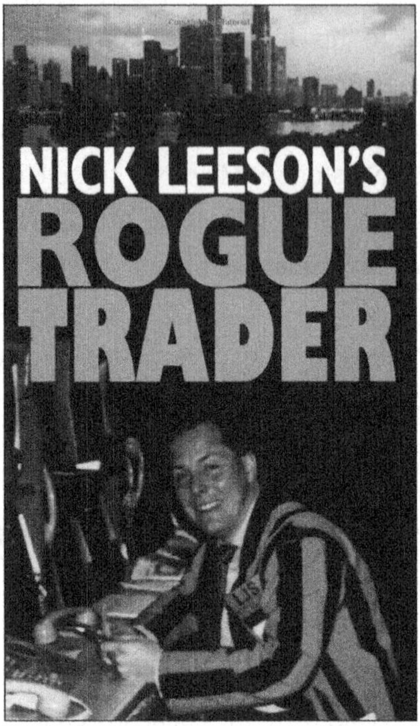

Book cover of the Rogue Trader; Source: Wikipedia

The Bank of England also messed up. The capital of Barings was only £250 million and I had £500 million of it. I know I failed my math A-level, but even I could add that sum. They allowed Barings to send over 100 percent of the bank's capital to me in Singapore when the legal limit was only 20 percent. [Barings] Treasury used to make me daily payments of between US$50 million and US$100 million without any logical reason. The basic rule of futures and options is that it is a cash-rich business and you receive more money than you pay to the exchange. The treasury also had to break down the reasons for their subsidiary lending to the Bank of England. The nonsensical reasons that I was giving them were passed on to the Bank of England.

The bank had, by the end of 1994, basically exhausted all their credit lines with other banks and didn't have any more money to give me. Now, you would think they would look at the situation and investigate. Barings management did quite the opposite. They went to the market and issued a bond for £100 million. As soon as the management received it, they sent it to me in Singapore.'

Leeson was released from prison on 3 July 1999.

At Harry's Bar, his release was commemorated. 'We held a "Flight of Freedom" party,' recalled Harry's Bar manager, Mr. Andrew Koh[8]. 'We served free beer for two hours and all the staff had T-shirts printed with the words, "Leeson Learns His Lesson". We half hoped that Nick might drop in for a drink but he didn't of course, he was whisked off by the authorities.'

8 *Leeson's legacy lives on in Singapore*, 23 February 2005, *BBC World Asia Report.*

10. The Tom Yum Effect

The 1987 market crisis was the driver of many of the market reforms across the globe during the 1990's. Asian markets also made substantial changes implementing the G-30 recommendations. But the strengths of the markets were very soon put to vigorous test with the financial crisis between June 1997 and January 1998 that swept through the 'tiger economies' of Southeast Asia like a brush fire.

It all started from Thailand.

Over the previous decade, Thailand together with the Southeast Asian economies of Malaysia, Singapore, Indonesia, Hong Kong, and South Korea, had registered some of the most impressive growth rates in the world. Thailand's growth in the first half of the 1990s averaged over 8%, before slowing to 6.4% in 1996. Although the inflation rate rose from 3.4% in 1993 to 5.9% in 1996, it was still moderate by the standards of emerging markets. Thailand's domestic savings were high - about 34% of GDP - and the government had fiscal surpluses in nine of the past ten years. With a fast-growing economy in a fast-growing region, Thailand was a free-market success story.

Bangkok, where most of the growth was concentrated, was awash in money and prosperity. As the Thai Baht was pegged to the US Dollar, banks and big corporations borrowed US Dollars at a lower rate and converted into Baht for domestic lending, leading to a credit boom. Above the proliferating wine bars and car showrooms, an overpowering new skyline emerged in Bangkok. Hundreds of imposing modern buildings filled with unsold space popped up in the city skyline enough to satisfy residential and commercial needs for many years. There was an immense property boom.

Restaurants, bars and lounges in the Silom and Sukhumvit districts were playing the pop beats and lyrics of Murray Head's '*One Night in Bangkok*':

Bangkok, oriental setting
And the city don't know what the city is getting ....
One night in Bangkok and the world's your oyster
The bars are temples but the pearls ain't free
You'll find a God in every golden cloister
A little flesh, a little history
I can feel an angel slidin' up to me
One night in Bangkok makes a hard man humble
Not much between despair and ecstasy ......

Murray Head's hit album; Source: Wikipedia

The impressive growth of the Thai economy fueled massive increases in foreign borrowing – government borrowing for infrastructure investment and corporate borrowing for investment expansion. However, the growth started to slow down in 1996 falling to 6.7% from 8.5% in the previous year, led by a sharp drop in exports due to the appreciation of the US Dollar to which the Baht was pegged. People became worried. The country was facing a budget deficit for the first time in a decade. The stock market dipped to eight-year lows, the trade deficit rose, and office vacancy rates in Bangkok exceeded 20% at the end of 1996. Bad property loans were putting pressure on the financial sector. Bangkok Bank of Commerce, which incurred over US$3 billion in bad loans, had to be taken over by the government in May 1996.

Pressure on the Baht to depreciate was starting to mount, but the Bank of Thailand (BOT) resisted depreciation as it would deepen the US Dollar debt burden of Thai corporations which had their currency exposure unhedged. A weaker Baht would also increase inflation.

Foreign currency traders were aware that Thailand's enormous external debt was denominated in US Dollars and would require a large demand of Dollars to finance the external debt. They believed the Baht was overvalued at 25 to the Dollar and need to fall sharply. They borrowed Baht from local banks and immediately resold them in the foreign-exchange markets for Dollar. If the Baht did weaken, they would buy the Baht back and pay off the loan and make a profit on the Dollar appreciation.

The Quantum Fund operated by George Soros was among the bigger speculators involved in selling the currency short, hoping to profit from an anticipated decline in its value. The hedge fund was reported to be involved in a US$4 billion bet that the currency would fall sharply, a strategy he employed to reap great profit in the early 1990's shorting the British Pound.

In his book, *Open Society: Reforming Global Capitalism,* Soros said: 'But I would not have been able to speculate [against the Baht] if the Thai economy or its financial system were not in such bad shape.'

He argued that hedge funds did not start the crisis, although they played a role in the turmoil. If a trend is unsustainable, it is surely better if it is reversed sooner rather than later, he said.

The BOT intervened and fought the currency war by purchasing Baht in the foreign-exchange market with US Dollars, and also raising interest rates to increase the attractiveness of the Baht to make it more costly for speculators to borrow Baht to sell in foreign currency markets. Measures were also adopted to restrict foreigners' access to Baht.

But in the course of this currency war, BOT found its reserves depleted very quickly as sentiment shifted against the Baht. Thailand's foreign-exchange reserves fell from US$37.2 billion in December 1996 to US$30.9 billion in June 1997 (prior to the Baht float). In addition, it was reported in August 1997 to have incurred off-balance-sheet obligations to deliver US$23.4 billion Dollars in the forward market over a twelve-month period. The foreign currency reserves were at the risk of being depleted. The battle peaked in mid-May 1997 when fourteen speculators bet a total of US$10 billion against the Baht to destroy the currency peg system.

The higher interest rates also raised the cost of borrowing and adversely affected floating-rate loan liabilities of the foreign debts.

On 2 July 1997, the Thai coalition government led by Prime Minister Chavalit decided to float the currency which had been pegged at 25 Baht to the Dollar. Very quickly it dropped to 33 Baht to the Dollar (a 50% drop) and continued to slide all the way to 57 Baht to the Dollar.

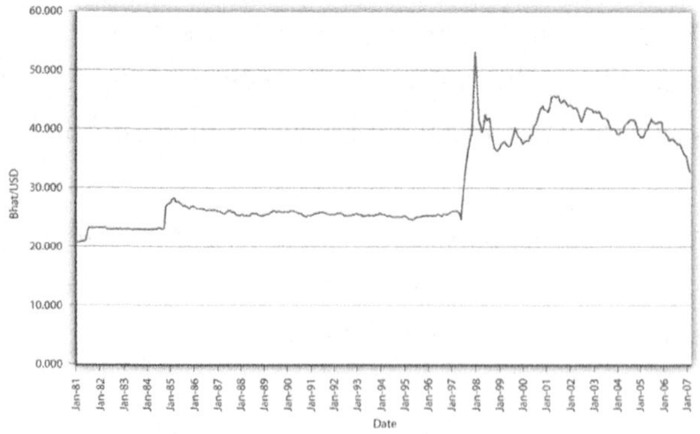

Thai Baht in big slide; Source: Wikipedia

Thai corporations and individuals, who held more than US$70 billion in foreign debt, equivalent to about half of the country's economic output, found their debt in Thai Baht had more than doubled and became bankrupt.

The crash of the Baht created a domino effect and resulted in the crash of all other currencies and stock markets in the region one by one. In some countries, the financial and economic problems also triggered social and political upheavals.

Thai workers in protest; *Source: Wikipedia*

When the dust started to settle in January 1998, the stock markets in many Southeast Asian countries had lost over 70% of their value, their currencies had depreciated against the US Dollar by a similar amount, and the once proud leaders of these countries were forced to go cap in hand to the International Monetary Fund to beg for massive financial assistance and accept its bitter medicine.

What was at the time perceived to be a localised currency and financial crisis in Thailand made its pungent, sour and spicy Tom Yum effect across the region.

Appendix: Timeline of the Thai Baht Crisis

February 1997	Trading in the shares of Finance One was suspended while the government tried to arrange for the troubled company to be acquired by a small Thai bank, in a deal sponsored by the Thai central bank. By this time, it was clear that bad loans in the Thai property market were swelling daily and had risen to over US$30 billion. Finance One was bankrupt and it was feared that others would follow.
April, 8 1997	Moody's drops Thailand's ratings 5 notches on evaporation of reserves
May 14, 1997	Thailand, with the intervention of Singapore, spends billions of Dollars of its foreign reserves to defend the Thai Baht against speculative attacks.
June 30, 1997	Prime Minister Chavalit Yongchaiyudh said that he would not devalue the Baht. This was the spark that ignited the Asian financial crisis as the Thai government failed to defend the Baht, which was pegged to the US Dollar.
July 2, 1997	Thailand devalues the Baht. News of the devaluation drops the value of the Baht by as much as 20% – a record low. The Thai government requests technical assistance from the International Monetary Fund (IMF).

August 5, 1997	Thailand agrees to adopt tough economic measures proposed by the IMF in return for a US$17 billion loan from the international lender and Asian nations. The Thai government closes forty-two ailing finance companies and imposes tax hikes as part of the IMF's insistence on austerity.
September 3, 1997	S&P drops Thailand's ratings 4 notches on evaporation of reserves.
Dec. 8, 1997	The Thai government announces that it will close fifty-six insolvent finance companies as part of the IMF's economic restructuring plan. 30,000 white-collar workers lose their jobs. Michel Camdessus, the IMF's managing director, praises Thailand for solid progress.

Source: http://historysquared.com/

11. The Gold Collection Drive

Seoul's commercial district today is always alive and busy. K-pop and Korean drama are wildly popular in the whole of Asia. Electronic products from Samsung and LG have become the choice of household consumers around the world. It's hard to believe that less than twenty years ago South Korea teetered on the brink of bankruptcy.

South Korea was one of the countries worst hit by the Asian financial crisis, with its economy going under by contracting over 8% in real terms in one year.

During the 1990's, Korea was one of the world's fastest growing economies with an average annual growth rate of 7-9% and a modest inflation rate of about 5% a year for the three years leading up to the crisis. The ratio of its foreign debt to GDP was less than 30%, the lowest among developing countries and less than that of many industrially advanced countries. In addition, the government's budget was balanced.

The Korean economy's growth had traditionally been dependent on large conglomerates or *chaebol*, the Korean version of Japanese *zaibatsu's*. Ever since the time of President Park Chung-Hee, Korean banks, under the explicit directive of the Korean government, had been lending to chaebols at preferential interest rates. They were minimally regulated because of their influence on Korean politics. There was a haste to build chaebols to compete on the world stage. The collusion between the banks, the government and the chaebols combined with lax regulation led to some chaebols being highly leveraged for aggressive expansions.

Meanwhile, Korea's current account balance started to deteriorate because of rising inflation, appreciation of the Korean Won, and the recession of the world economy. In order to finance the growing current account deficits, the government encouraged capital inflows. Meanwhile, as part of the requirements for joining OECD (Organisation for Economic Co-operation and Development) in 1996, the government implemented financial deregulation and capital market opening. But it chose to liberalise short-term capital inflows ahead of long-term capital inflows. This led to banks and businesses financing long-term investments with short-term foreign borrowings especially in US Dollars and Japanese Yen. In the banking sector, short-term external debts accounted for 61% of total external debts in 1996, creating maturity as well as currency mismatches.

From mid-1995, Washington reversed its policy to strengthen the US Dollar, particularly against the Japanese Yen. As the US Dollar weighed heavily in the price determination of the Korean Won under the managed float system, the Won failed to depreciate as much as the Yen. In addition, Korean exports were competing directly with Japanese in international markets. As the Dollar became stronger against the Japanese Yen, Korea not only experienced an accelerated increase in its trade deficit, but also a severe drop in the profitability of investments undertaken for exports. Some chaebols started to run into financial difficulties and non-performing loans at Korean banks sharply increased, thus undermining the financial soundness of Korean domestic banking institutions.

In January 1997, the Hanbo group experienced serious financial difficulty, ultimately ending in bankruptcy. In July 1997, South Korea's third largest car maker, Kia Motors, asked for emergency loans from the government for a bail-out.

Meanwhile, the currency crisis of Southeast Asian countries which started in Thailand in May continued to deepen and soon developed into a region-wide contagion. In late October 1997, Hong Kong was under speculative attack on its currency peg followed by a sharp decline in the stock market.

With the whole region in difficulty, foreign creditors, particularly American and Japanese banks, refused to roll over their loans to Korean financial institutions. This almost caused a bank run in Korea, and the Korean Won depreciated over 25% in value. This in turn forced the Korean government to use its limited foreign currency reserves to help Korean financial institutions honour their short-term obligations. In this process, a substantial portion of the nation's US$25 foreign reserves was advanced to the overseas branches of Korean banks. This quickly reduced the nation's usable foreign reserves to a dangerous level.

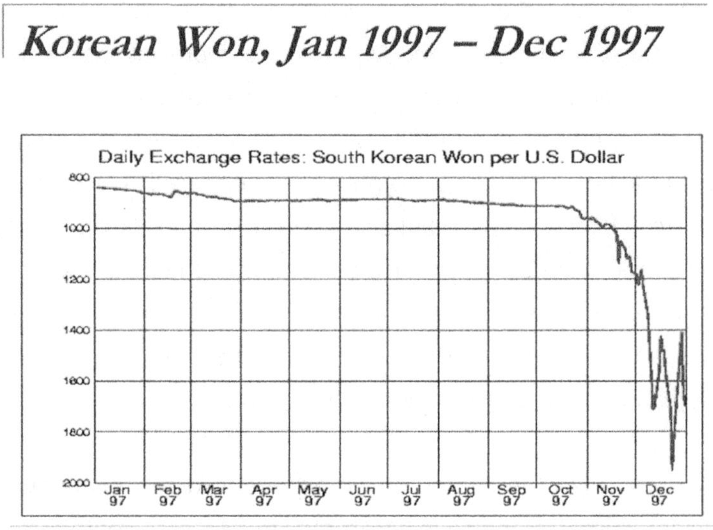

Korean Won in sharp fall; Source: Wikipedia

The Seoul Stock Exchange fell by 4% on 7 November 1997, It plunged another 7% on 8 November, its biggest one-day drop to that date. As the withdrawal of foreign funds accelerated, on 21 November the Korean government officially requested help from the IMF. And on 24

November, the stock market fell a further 7.2% in fear of some strict terms imposed by IMF. On 28 November 1997, Moody's lowered the credit ratings of South Korea from A1 to A3, and on 11 December downgraded again to B2.

The crisis in Korea was a liquidity crisis due to serious mismatches in maturity, in currency, and in the capital structure in the balance sheets of the financial and non-financial sectors of the economy. A rapid infusion of hard currency reserves was critical more than anything else. However, what the IMF and the Korean government agreed upon on 3 December 1997 was far from this. The total amount of money that the IMF together with other international financial institutions offered to bail out Korea was US$58.4 billion with very tough conditions attached. Out of this, US$23.4 billion was reserved as a second line of defence that would be made available to Korea by G-7 countries only if the initial amount of US$35 billion contributed by the IMF and other multilateral institutions proved inadequate. The disbursement of the US$35 billion was to be spread over more than two years until the year 2000, with each instalment conditioned upon the progress Korea was to make in structural reforms and the further tightening of its monetary and fiscal policies.

It is worth noting that the amount Korea was allowed to withdraw, immediately after reaching agreement with the IMF on 3 December, was US$5.6 billion. Korea was allowed to withdraw an additional US$3.5 billion on 18 December. Thus, the total amount Korea was able to withdraw during this fifteen-day period was only US$9.1 billion.

Foreign banks did not believe these amounts from IMF were adequate in meeting the nation's short-term obligations. Refusal on loan rollovers continued, and Korea's limited foreign reserves were rapidly depleted. An internal memorandum prepared by the Bank of Korea on 18 December, taking into account both the inflows of foreign funds expected during the ensuing twelve-day period, plus the foreign reserve balance on hand and the outflows expected to take place during the same period, showed that the foreign reserve balance expected on 31 December would be anywhere from negative US$600 million to positive US$900 million.

Foreign creditors further accelerated the withdrawal of their funds from Korea, pushing the country to the verge of a sovereign default less than two weeks after the initial agreement was signed. On 19 December, at the Korean government's request, the US government persuaded the IMF to quickly enter into a new round of negotiations with Korea for a further front-loading of bail-out money, and also exerted its influence on the financial institutions of G-7 countries to roll over their short-term credits to Korea for one month. In return for this favour, the Korean government and foreign banks reached an agreement on 28 January 1998 that led to restructuring nearly 95% of Korea's short-term debt by 18 March 1998. In rescheduling these debts, foreign banks charged extraordinarily high interest rates, ranging from 2.25% to 2.75% points above the then prevailing six-month LIBOR (London Interbank Offer Rate) interest rate of 5.66%.

With the success of the rollover and the maturity extension and the authorities' moves to implement financial and corporate reform programmes, the market's view on Korea improved dramatically. The Dollar/Won exchange rate, which recorded an all-time high of 1,965 on 24 December 1997, declined to a range of 1,600-1,800 in January 1998, 1,400 by the end of March, and then stayed at 1,200 Won at the end of 1998.

Two things about the way South Korea faced the Asian Financial Crisis were remarkable.

First was the speed with which the country rebuilt its economy. The government quickly got on with implementing post-crisis economic and financial reforms. Despite an initial sharp economic slowdown and numerous corporate bankruptcies, it has managed to triple its per capital GDP in Dollar terms in the following ten years. Its financial sector has become one of the region's strongest, combining greater openness with better regulation. A crisis among over-extended credit-card lenders in 2003 had almost no contagious effect on the broader financial system. In addition, its economy has become more transparent and flexible, interest rates are lower, and foreign reserves have risen massively.

The second was Korean's shared sense of national purpose and a willingness to sacrifice individual comfort to toil hard with a single mind to get the country out of the crisis. The voluntary, public self-sacrifice of the Korean people helped Korea to repay its IMF loan ahead of schedule, after just three years.

The Koreans took on themselves very bitterly the extremely harsh belt-tightening measures imposed by the IMF, so much so that they called it the 'IMF Crisis' as if it was caused by the IMF. The IMF reform programmes were humiliating to the country. Many Koreans viewed the crisis as fueled by foreign speculators driving down the value of their currency, foreign lenders prematurely calling in their loans, and a foreign IMF that did not care about the businesses they drove into bankruptcy, the people laid off from their jobs or the dreams of the people that all this sudden hardship destroyed. Some desperate families, in dire economic straits, left their children at orphanages and these kids were called IMF orphans. The acronym IMF in Korea became a symbol of every malaise that the country was going through at the time. It literally became a new word in the Korean vocabulary - IMF was cynically referred to an acronym of "I'm Fired" by the local media.

Koreans protesting against IMF; Source: AFP

The Koreans acknowledged that it would get worse before it would get better and prepared for the same by endorsing the harsh economic reforms that the government undertook. With the tripartite consensus of the government, the corporations and the labour unions, a company's power to lay off workers was codified in the Labour Standard Act. 1.7 million of Koreans lost their jobs in the readjustment of the labour markets. Those who retained their jobs worked twice the hours to produce more. They spent less and saved more. Government employees agreed to give 10% of their salary to create a fund to provide for those who have lost their jobs.

This sense of shared burden is epitomised in the gold jewelry donations. Starting in January 1998, the government asked the country's citizens to donate their gold jewelry to help repay the loan more quickly. Millions answered the call and went to special collection points to give the government what they could in heirlooms, wedding rings or small gold figures, such as those traditionally presented in Korea on a child's first birthday. Athletes brought in gold medals and trophies.

Korean house-wives spontaneously participated in gold donation campaign to save the country from economic crisis; Source: Wikipedia

'These things are connected with beautiful memories and very precious,' said Kyoung Sung-Suk, then a student and now a visiting professor of Korean studies at the University of Bonn. My parents were among those who donated the gold jewelry they had received as gifts on my first birthday.[9]

'To think of all the gold and the memories that we had to give away,' said Choi Gwang-Ja, who like many other South Korean women gave away her gold jewelry to help dig the national economy out of the financial crisis.

'It's really heart-breaking. And it makes me fill with tears even now, because each piece of jewelry had a story - it was my wedding ring, my husband's wedding ring, it was the ring given to me when my daughter was born,' she says. 'But at the time, it was the only thing we could do. People were saying that the whole country was going bankrupt.'[10]

---

9 *Koreans' gold donations - a model for Greeks?* 2 April 2015, *http://www.dw.com/*

10 *What Eurozone countries can learn from South Korea,* 9 July 2012, *BBC News Seoul*

Korea's gold collection drive was featured in many foreign media outlets all across the world. The result was impressive. Within months, 227 tonnes of gold were collected, equivalent to a quarter ounce for every adult in South Korea, valued at more than US$3 billion, according to a report in Hankyoreh newspaper!

12. Battle against Hedge Funds

1997 was a historic year, remembered for the official transfer of the British sovereignty of Hong Kong to the People's Republic of China. The handover ceremony, commencing on the drizzling night of 30 June 1997 and finishing on 1 July 1997, was televised internationally. It was dubbed by Prince Charles in his diary 'The Great Chinese Takeaway'[11].

But 1997 also set the stage for an epic battle by Hong Kong in defence of its currency against the hedge funds and speculators.

The Hong Kong Dollar had been pegged at 7.8 to the US Dollar since October 1983 during the period of difficult Sino-British negotiations over the future of Hong Kong, which resulted in waves of massive capital flight. There was a rapid deterioration in market confidence in the local economy at this time. This sentiment led to a sharp collapse of the Hong Kong Dollar, by 13% in just two days to a record low point of 9.6 per US Dollar. Worried Hong Kong people scrambled for groceries and food staples. Even toilet paper became a target of panic buying. On 15 October 1983, the Hong Kong government announced linking the local currency to the greenback, taking the suggestion from John Greenwood, an economist of Invesco, in an article he wrote for the Asian Monetary Monitor. The currency peg provided an external anchor, and the Hong Kong Dollar was stabilised.

But the peg came under severe speculative pressure in October 1997 because Hong Kong's inflation rate had been significantly higher than the U.S. Hedge funds such as Quantum, Tiger, Omega and others began their attack in October 1997 after acquiring huge

11 *Charles sues Mail for printing his 'waxworks' jibe at Chinese leaders*, 19 November 2015, *The Guardian*.

amounts of Hong Kong Dollars from the money market. They firstly established short positions in Hang Seng Index futures and then began to borrow shares from banks and securities firms. Then they started short selling in the stock market and spreading rumours that, with all the countries in Asia devaluing their currencies, the Hong Kong government would have no choice but to let its currency depreciate so as to maintain its competitiveness. All these actions created a panic for the public as well as genuine foreign investors.

After seeing the financial meltdown in other Asian countries, the public investors including investment funds began to feel uneasy and started to unload their holdings thus creating a crash in the stock market. Between 20 and 23 October the Hang Seng Index dropped 23%. When the Hong Kong stock market looked like following their Asian neighbours' footsteps, the Hong Kong Dollar began to feel tremendous pressure from short selling. This immediately increased the pressure in Hong Kong Dollar money market. On 23 October 1997, when the speculative attack was at its fiercest, overnight Hong Kong Dollar was pushed up to as much as 250% to borrow. The benchmark three-month Hong Kong Interbank Offer Rate (HIBOR) was fixed at 37%, while six-month Hong Kong Dollar funding stood at 33%.

At this moment, hedge funds started to lend out the borrowed Hong Kong Dollar in the money market and enjoyed a huge profit on the interest rate differential. While the Hong Kong government were busy defending the Hong Kong Dollar peg, the hedge funds started to square off their Hang Seng Index futures short positions, bought back the short-selling shares from the stock market and declared a windfall profit in this operation, leaving the Hong Kong government with a big hole in its financial market.

Hong Kong Dollar under speculative pressure; Source: Wikipedia

The Hong Kong Monetary Authority (HKMA), the city's de facto central bank, spent more than US$1 billion to defend the local currency. With more than US$80 billion in foreign reserves, equivalent to 700% of its M1 money supply and 45% of its M3 money supply, the HKMA was able to hold the peg.

To strengthen its defence of the Hong Kong Dollar peg with the US Dollar, the HKMA improved its efficiency in monitoring the banks' Hong Kong Dollar movement. The government continued to operate its stock market, financial futures and money market normally, but this policy continually invited further attacks by the hedge funds. It was especially apparent between June and August 1998, during which time hedge funds shorted Hang Seng Index futures to profit from the pegged currency system. Each time when the hedge funds attacked, no matter how efficient the monitoring system was, the hedge funds would easily make money out of it by using the same old tricks.

In late July to early August 1998, Japan announced worse than expected economic data. The Yen was fiercely attacked by foreign-exchange speculators and dropped from 135 per US Dollar to 147. Hedge funds saw this as a great opportunity to break the Hong Kong Dollar peg. This round they combined all the forces that they could gather, including small and big hedge funds, mutual funds and some big foreign banks. They started borrowing Hong Kong Dollar heavily in the money market, taking in about HK$100 billion from the money market at a rate between 8-10%. Subsequently, they started short selling Hang Seng Index futures when the index was about 8,500. They then borrowed HSBC, HK Telecom and other big blue-chip shares from foreign owners and securities firms.

In early August the war of the century began. Hedge funds started to spread rumours about the possible devaluation of China's RMB due to the weakness in Japanese Yen. They pushed down RMB exchange rate in the black market to create the necessity atmosphere. Then they started to attack the Hong Kong Dollar by, firstly, short-selling Hong Kong Dollar in the foreign-exchange market. Secondly, they sold down Hang Seng futures index towards 7,500 levels. Thirdly, they spread rumours that the Hong Kong government would soon have to unpeg the HK Dollar. Under normal circumstances, this three-pronged attack would have created a panic in the stock market and a shot up in domestic interest rate.

The HKMA, led by the then Financial Secretary, Donald Tsang, decided to counter-attack against the speculators at this point. First, it bought about HK$35 billion from the foreign-exchange market using its US Dollar reserves. By doing so, it managed to stabilise HK Dollar exchange rate and at the same time indirectly pumped HK Dollar into the money market, which prevented the shortage of HK Dollar in the market and therefore eased off the interest rate.

Seeing what was happening in the money market, hedge funds started to use media and rating agencies to spread rumours about the worsening of Hong Kong economy and the inevitable unpeg on currency. The stock market continued to be jittered by the tense environment and on 13 August, Hang Seng Index plunged to a new low and closed at 6,660. Hedge funds thought that while they might not be able to make money in the foreign-exchange and money market, they could still make a windfall profit in short-selling shares and the futures index. They were confident that the Hang Seng Index would drop to their targeted level of 5,500 in the next few days and started counting their profit - without realising that Hong Kong government was preparing for the second wave of counter-attack.

On 14 August, the Hong Kong government began its intervention in the stock and futures markets simultaneously. First, it started heavily buying blue chips like HSBC and HK Telecom in the stock market. In order not to let the hedge funds know in advance, it bought the shares through UK, China and Hong Kong brokerage firms so as to give an impression that the buying of shares came from general investment funds. On this day, Hong Kong government used about HK$4 billion to buy shares and the Hang Seng Index shot up 574 points at close. This had caught hedge funds off-guard and the Hong Kong government only announced its intervention after the market closed. Most of the hedge funds were still holding their short positions and had to top-up margin in Hang Seng Index futures.

In view of the adverse position running against him, on 16 August, Soros decided to create negative news to pull down the market. He took the opportunity and announced that Russia should devalue the Rouble so as to rescue its economy. The next day, on 17 August, markets in U.S. and Europe reacted to Soros' advice and plunged. 17 August was a Hong Kong public holiday. Hedge funds were expecting that, after a plunge in Europe and U.S., on 18 August when Hang Seng started trading, it would probably drop 1,000 points. However, the Hong Kong government continued to intervene in the market and to their surprise Hang Seng only dropped a mere 13 points.

During the following six days, the battle between hedge funds and the Hong Kong government continued; hedge funds continued shorting the market and the Hong Kong government remained the main buyer. At the same time, hedge funds used the media to spread news against the Hong Kong Dollar peg. The Hong Kong government also used the same tactics of hedge funds, spreading the rumour through local media and broking firms that it had amassed HK$1 trillion (backed by China's reserves) to combat the speculators. It then asked trusted fund managers not to lend shares to hedge funds for short selling and invited big local tycoons to join hands in buying shares. The battle was very fierce and market continued to see-saw up and down.

Both hedge funds and the Hong Kong government knew very well that the final battle that would decide the ultimate winner would only come at the expiry date of the August Hang Seng future index. On that date, most of the futures contracts would have to close out, roll over or cash settle. To prepare for the finale, the Hong Kong government started to do spread trades in Hang Seng futures index. It aggressively bought the August contracts and sold the same quantity for the September month; this action widened the spread between the two months' contracts, whereby September contract was now much lower than the August contract. The purpose was to make a rollover by the hedge funds of their short positions more costly for them, thereby forcing them to close out in August. As a result, most of the smaller hedge funds had no choice but to square off their positions and left the market. The only players now hanging on in the battle field were big hedge funds such as Quantum, Tiger and Omega.

On 27 August, hedge funds launched their attack. They sold a total of HK$20 billion in the stock market and at the same time sent the chief investment strategist of Quantum Fund to announce in the press that the Hong Kong government would surely lose, claiming that hedge funds would never fight a no-win battle. The hedge funds were hoping to use the press to create a psychological edge to attract other speculators to join them to sell the next day.

The next day, 28 August, was the finale of the battle. Both sides had gathered a huge amount of ammunition hoping to kill off the other side. The day saw record trading of HK$79 billion (almost US$10 billion), about fifteen times average daily turnover.

The Hang Seng Index closed at 7,829, down just 1.18% for the day, and up from 6,600 when the massive government interventions began on 14 August. It was a day dubbed D-Day in Hong Kong by the *Hong Kong Standard*.

As the dust of battle settled on 28 August, Donald Tsang was reported saying to the press: 'We have frustrated their plan......That is a deterrent, but that does not mean they will not come back. We want to tell them we will not sit with folded arms.'[12] He pledged further government measures to beef up regulations aimed at protecting the territory against fresh speculative attacks.

In this financial battle, the Hong Kong government had committed as much as US$10 billion of Hong Kong's US$96 billion reserves. It ended up holding approximately HK$120 billion (US$15 billion) worth of shares in various companies, and became the largest shareholder of some of those companies, e.g. 10% of HSBC.

Costly as this victory might have been, it was a turning point in the war against hedge funds and speculators in the Asian financial crisis. The Hong Kong government had achieved the following:

- A gain of an estimated HK$1.6 billion in this operation, which included the transactions done in August and the open positions marked to current market price.

- Holding substantial short contracts in September Hang Seng futures index, which could be used for protecting the downward movement in futures index in case hedge funds attack again.

- Holding substantial amount of HSBC and HK Telecom shares, and becoming the second major shareholder of a number of other blue chip counters, which would make borrowing for short selling by hedge funds more difficult in future.

- Successfully defended the crash in the stock market and hence prevented a sharp downturn in its economy in the third quarter.

---

12 *Hong Kong battles recession and speculators*, 28 August 1998, *BBC News*.

As for hedge funds, the myth that they were invincible was dispelled. But while they had lost the battle, the actual financial results were not exactly that hurtful. Most of their short positions were established when Hang Seng was around 8,000 to 8,500 level. After netting off with the previous attacks, they were actually still in profit.

The battle was settled, but what about the war? Hong Kong was a global icon of *laissez-faire* capitalism usually adopting a policy of positive non-interventionism, but the Hong Kong government's move to buy up blue-chip stocks to maintain the market level was characterised by one foreign trader as 'the re-nationalisation of Hong Kong'. Its actions came under especially heavy criticism from international investors in the western world who saw Hong Kong as turning its back on free-market philosophy. In international circles, wrote Salomon Smith Barney analyst Anil Daswani shortly after the intervention, 'Hong Kong's reputation as one of the world's leading free markets has been shattered'.

On 29 August, the *South China Morning Post* commented in its editorial: 'It may turn out that Donald Tsang has pulled off one of the great investment coups in history.... Of more immediate concern, however, is what he will do now. . .. For the past two trading days, the government was virtually the only buyer on the market. . .. Around the world investment funds scoured their vaults for Hong Kong stock to sell into this buying campaign on the reasoning that it cannot last and prices will drop when it ends'.

Edgar Cheng, former Chairman of the Hong Kong Stock Exchange, countered the complaints, of those decrying the Hong Kong government's intervention in the markets, in a letter to the editor of the *South China Business Post* on 26 August. Cheng noted: '.... those who introduced antitrust legislation in the United States and elsewhere considered that forceful intervention by the state was not only justified but necessary to protect markets from enslavement by a small number of powerful market players......At the end of the day, whether the Hong Kong government's intervention in the stock market is considered "right" or "wrong" will be determined by whether it succeeds in achieving its objective. To condemn it on the grounds that it offends against the philosophy of free markets is humbug'.

Soros praised Hong Kong for blocking his attack in an interview with *China Central Television* years later. 'They actually did a very good job defending the Hong Kong Dollar, so they deserve credit. And my attack, if you call it that, was without success', he said. 'I don't feel any sense of guilt .... There is nothing wrong about it. This is a point people have difficulty understanding because, in speculating in the financial markets, I do so according to the rules that prevail.'[13]

In an interview with the *China Business News* in 2007, the former managing director of Soros Fund Management, Rodney Jones, admitted in hindsight: '[The Hong Kong] Government intervention raised public confidence in the market when it was near total collapse. It prevented a bigger crisis and saved the market'.[14]

The buying spree by the Hong Kong government, however, left an enormous overhang of illiquidity in the market in the following months. The Exchange Fund Investment Limited, established in October 1998 by the Hong Kong government, sought advice from the financial industry on how to dispose of the massive holding of Hong Kong stocks in an orderly manner. Several proposals were considered but the idea of a stock-neutral solution such as an exchange-traded index fund (ETF) that would create minimal disruption to the market was most attractive.

13 Soros *praises HK for blocking his Dollar 'attacks'*, 16 June 2009, *South China Morning Post.*

14 *Soros manager regrets attack on HK Dollar*, 5 July 2007, *China Business News*

A RFP (Request for Proposal) was issued inviting custodian banks to pitch for the appointment as trustee and custodian for the ETF to be set up. I was at The Bank of New York at that time and worked with several colleagues from the U.S. with experience servicing SPDR exchange-traded funds, answering the RFP and presenting in the beauty parade. The mandate ultimately went to the one-stop-shop solution with State Street Global Advisors Asia Ltd as the fund manager and State Street Bank and Trust as the trustee and custodian. In November 1999, the Tracker Fund of Hong Kong was launched. It marked the birth of the first publicly-traded ETF in Hong Kong as well as the first in Asia.

Hong Kong Tracker Fund advertisement; Source: youtube.com

In disposing of its massive stock holdings, the Hong Kong government ultimately made a profit of about HK$30 billion (US$4 billion).

13. The Capital Control

Within days of the Thai Baht devaluation in July 1997, the Malaysian Ringgit was heavily traded by speculators, notably Soros's Quantum Fund and other hedge funds. They borrowed the Ringgit in offshore markets and sold it down repeatedly, thus greatly devaluing the currency. To make matters worse, they also began to dump Malaysian shares and to short-sell.

Bank Negara Malaysia (BNM), the central bank, tried to defend the Ringgit by making active interventions in the foreign-exchange market. It also pushed the overnight rate from under 8% to over 40% to make it costly to borrow the currency. But rather than achieving a rebound, the higher rates helped cause a recession. The Ringgit lost about a third of its value against the Dollar in twelve months. This led to credit ratings downgrades and a general sell-off on the stock and currency markets.

At the World Bank Forum held in Hong Kong in September 1997, the then Prime Minister of Malaysia, Dr. Mahathir Mohammad, said before the conference: 'All these [Asian] countries have spent forty years trying to build up their economies, and a moron like Soros comes along with a lot of money and undermines them.'[15]

Soros denied that he had a role in devaluing the Ringgit. In his own speech, he said that ironically the buying of Malaysian currency by his Fund during the crash helped buffer the impact. Mahathir, he claimed, was using him as a scapegoat for his own mistakes.

---

15 *Malaysian Leader, Soros Trade Barbs*, 22 September 1997, *Los Angeles Times*.

Soros speaking at World Economic Forum; Source: commons.wikimedia.org

By the end of 1997, the country ratings of Malaysia had fallen many notches from investment grade to junk, the Kuala Lumpur Stock Exchange (KLSE) had lost more than 50% from above 1,200 to under 600, and the Ringgit had lost 50% of its value, falling from above 2.50 to under 4.57 to the Dollar on 23 January 1998. It was clear that the series of measures were not working.

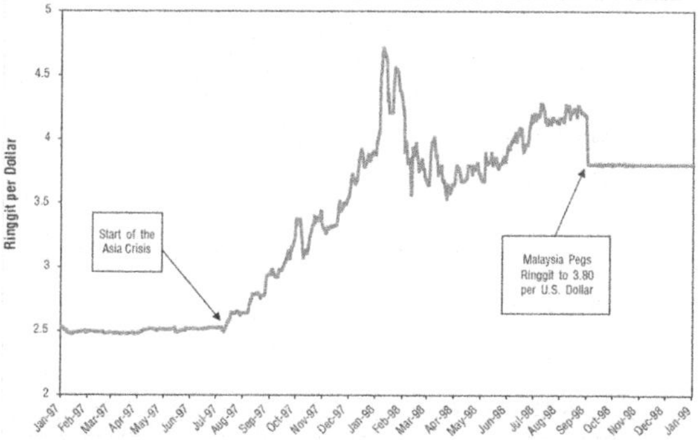

Malaysian Ringgit in free fall; Source: Wikipedia

Desperate situations needed desperate measures. A National Economic Action Council (NEAC) was formed in January 1998 with the executive power to override all red tape and jurisdiction of different ministries for the implementation of measures to address the situation. The NEAC had been secretly toying with the idea of capital control for several months, but this was ardently opposed by the BNM who argued that other countries that had adopted capital control found their future capital raising in the international markets shunned by investors and had to pay high costs of funding. Some members of the NEAC also found difficulty in supporting the proposal.

The chief architect of Malaysia's capital control was Nor Mohamed Yakcop, the Finance Minister. He was formerly running the foreign-exchange trading desk in BNM and during his reign BNM lost more than RM30 billion during the 1992 European Financial Crisis by purchasing large amount of the Sterling in the hope that it would appreciate when floated, while Soros made his reputation as the man who broke The Bank of England by shorting the Sterling.

The idea of capital control was originated during Mahathir's trip to Argentina. While in Argentina, Mahathir called upon Nor Mohamed Yakcop to enlighten him on the inner workings of the foreign-exchange market. He then asked Nor Mohamed Yakcop to design the country's capital-control policy, who then went through the country's Balance of Payments report line by line looking for any leakages to prevent any capital outflow from the country. Argentina and other Latin American countries were the experts in capital control. There were a lot of handy measures to borrow.

On 1 September 1998, after the Asian financial crisis had devastated other countries for more than a year, Mahathir announced capital control with a package of measures designed to stabilise the Ringgit and to control the capital flows:

- Overseas bound local travellers are only allowed to take up to RM1,000.

- Remittance of funds by residents to overseas are capped at RM10,000.

- Ringgit is pegged to the Dollar at the rate of RM3.80 to US$1 to facilitate trade in the domestic sector.

- Any Ringgit remains outside of Malaysia considered not legal tender.

- Any credit facilities obtained overseas need to seek approval first and only companies that earn foreign-exchange are allowed to obtain offshore credit.

- Funds raised from the sale of equities or other forms of investments need to remain in the country for twelve months.

- Clearing of stocks listed on the Kuala Lumpur Stock Exchange (KLSE) can only be done on the KLSE or its approved exchanges.

- RM500 and RM1000 currency notes are made non-legal tender to prevent smuggling of Ringgit to neighbouring countries.

- Dealing of shares in CLOB (Central Limit Order Book) was made illegal to prevent the flow of funds to Singapore and also discourage the arbitraging of shares between the two exchanges.

These measures were designed to kill the offshore Ringgit market, which was viewed as the source of speculative funds and upward pressure on domestic interest rates. The new measures required that all Ringgit held offshore be repatriated within a month, after which only the Ringgit already in Malaysia would be legal tender. Furthermore, Ringgit lending by Malaysians to foreigners was prohibited. With these regulatory measures, the offshore market for Ringgit was eliminated. As Nor Mohamed Yakcop said: 'It's easier to stop the guy who has the Ringgit from lending to currency speculators than it is to prevent speculators from borrowing Ringgit'.

Business Week likened the measures to a financial Roach Motel: 'Money can get in, but it can't get out'.[16] Mahathir was a medical doctor by training. He surely had strong know-how in stopping the flow of blood and oxygen supply to cancer cells in the system before cutting them off clinically.

The '*rojak*' of control measures, a teasing nickname used by the financial industry meaning '*the odd mix*' in Malay slang, was complicated to implement and caused a lot of confusion. It was a nightmare for the custody industry.

We suddenly had to support hundreds of clients to get approval for inbound and outbound movements of the Ringgit. But the control forms and other forms designed to track the movements of the Ringgit proved to be very confusing. For example, one of the conditions for funds raised from the sale of equities and other investments had to be remained in the country for a minimum of twelve months. It was not specified whether the residents and the locals were required to do so and consequently it created a lot of confusion. To the credit of the Malaysian government, the NEAC Communications Team was shortly formed to deal with the issues and to educate the industry and the public on the new measures. Step by step, the capital-control measures were put into order.

16 *Capital controls: Lifeline or Noose?* 28 September 1998, *Business Week*.

But the bigger nightmare was the overnight declaration that dealing of Malaysian shares on the CLOB was illegal. The over-the-counter market for shares on the KLSE had been set up in Singapore to trade Malaysian companies after the Malaysian and Singaporean exchanges separated in 1990. Over the years it had developed into a main avenue for Singaporean as well as foreign investors to invest in Malaysian equities. With the capital-control measure, having the CLOB investors' accounts frozen altogether and their claims declared invalid, some US$4.47 billion worth of shares were frozen, affecting 172,000 investors, 90% Singaporeans. That worked out to about US$25,000 per CLOB investor, indicating that these CLOB share buyers were not small fry and yet they got killed by events beyond their control. The *Economist* described it as '*Daylight Clobbery*' in an article in July 1999.

An ugly war of words ensued between the Malaysian and Singaporean market authorities. BNM claimed that during the Asian financial crisis, CLOB shares were being borrowed for short sale on the Malaysian market. It was further suggested that the Singapore authorities had done nothing to deter such damaging actions to the Malaysian market. The war of words then shifted over to the legitimacy of the CLOB market, with KLSE noting that the CLOB market was created unilaterally by the Stock Exchange of Singapore (SES) to generate revenue and was never endorsed by the Malaysian authorities, effectively an unauthorised market for Malaysian shares.

Many CLOB investors sold their shares after the Malaysian measures were announced, including 24,000 who sold all their Malaysian shares. All of them would have made substantial losses. I also lost several thousand Singapore Dollars with my personal investment in Malaysian stocks.

No clear resolution emerged until early 2000 when the two exchanges worked out a scheme of arrangement for letting CLOB investors trade out of their misery, where investors were offered two options, both of which involved releasing of CLOB shares on a staggered basis over ten months.

Malaysia was booted out of the MSCI Global Emerging-Market Index after imposing the controls. Mahathir was under severe criticism from his international critics and the global investment community. But his controversial measures had support from some prominent economists, including Paul Krugman of the Massachusetts Institute of Technology, who suggested Asian nations should consider the use of capital controls to shield their economies from more turmoil.

The capital control gradually brought stability to the economy - the exchange rate was stabilised and an offshore market for the Ringgit ceased to exist. The forced repatriation of funds from Singapore and other offshore markets resulted in more money being available for loans. It allowed Malaysia to lower interest rates in order to stimulate consumption and business activities. Major restructuring in the financial sector and the build-up of foreign-exchange reserves, to levels sufficient to finance more than eight months of retained imports, made Malaysia better equipped to deal with financial emergencies.

After the dust of the crisis had settled, the Malaysian government progressively dismantled the exchange and other controls imposed during the crisis, including abandoning the Ringgit peg to the US Dollar in July 2005 in favour of a managed float similar to the Singapore Dollar.

Mahathir was hailed for saving the country from the worst ravages of the Asian financial crisis and preserving the country's monetary and economic independence from the IMF's rescue aid to avoid much of the chaos that crippled the other South-East Asian economies.

Appendix: Timeline of Malaysian Currency Control

2 Jul 1997	Thailand decided to float the Baht
10 Jul1997	Bank Negara Malaysia intervened in the Forex market to defend the Ringgit.
13 Aug 1997	Mahathir attacked rogue speculators and pointed finger at Soros.
27 Aug 1997	Malaysia designated the 100 Index-linked counters and banned Short Selling.
4 Sep 1997	Malaysian Ringgit continued to plunge.
20 Sep 1997	Mahathir in Hong Kong called currency trading immoral and to be banned.
21 Sep 1997	Soros called Mahathir 'a menace to his country'.
2 Oct 1997	Mahathir and Nor Mohamed Yakcop visited Argentina and finalised Capital-control.
5 Dec 1997	Malaysia imposed tough market measures by Anwar Ibrahim.
7 Jan 1998	NEAC was formed.
16 Feb 1998	BNM reduced SRR (Statutory Reserve Requirement) from 13.5% to 10% in banks, boosting liquidity in banks.

20 May 1998	Asian currencies continued to plunge.
20 Jun 1998	Formation of Danaharta as an asset management company to handle NPLs.
10 Aug 1998	Danamodal was formed to recapitalise the Banking Sector.
16 Aug 1998	KLCI (Kuala Lumpur Composite Index) plunged to the lowest at 260 points.
1 Sep 1998	Imposition of Capital-control.

Source: '*Asian Financial Crisis Lessons: Can Malaysia's Capital-controls be Copied?*' *by Sam Chee Kong*

14. The Millennium Bug

The start of Year 2000 was a historical event for people around the world to celebrate and to rejoice for the beginning of a new millennium, but it was supposedly also the date of catastrophe for many others - all from a small assumption made years ago when computers were first being programmed.

The Y2K (Year 2000) problem existed because old computer software set aside only two date fields for year identification in computer code. Most dates were programmed to automatically assume that the date began with 19 as in 1977 or 1988 to save capacity in expensive data-storage hardware.

Though the problem had been identified by technology specialists for more than a decade prior to 2000, it was the late '90s that saw a frenzy of companies working to update their software.

The phrase Y2K first appeared in a TIME story in 1998 that explained the problem: 'The bug at the centre of the Year 2000 mess is fairly simple. In what's proving to be a ludicrously shortsighted shortcut, many system programmers set aside only two digits to denote the year in dates, as in 06/15/98 rather than 06/15/1998. Trouble is, when the computer's clock strikes 2000, the math can get screwy. Date-based equations like 2000 – 1997 = 3 become 00 – 97 = -97. That can prompt some computers to do the wrong thing and stop others from doing anything at all'.

According to computer experts, the Y2K problem can spread like an infection. Wrong information from old code is fed to millions of lines of new code from millions of lines of old code. The wrong information can come not only from computer code within a firm, but also from any of its hundreds of vendors or partners.

Given how much of our everyday lives was run by computers, the new year starting 1 January 2000 was expected to bring serious computer repercussions. Computers would be so confused that they would shut down completely. Airports, traffic lights, power grid, microwaves and televisions and much else - all of which were run by computers - were predicted to be affected by the Y2K bug.

The fear of a fallout was scary enough for *TIME* magazine to put the hysteria on its cover in the January 1999 issue under the headline 'The End of the World!?'!

Time magazine cover on Y2K; Source: Wikipedia

Custodians saw Y2K as an extreme risk to their operations. In 1998, we started fixing our internal systems for Y2K and in 1999 we were testing how our software would interact with vendors, clients and others right up to the millennium. A total of US$95 to 100 million was reported to have been budgeted for the Y2K problem by major custodians. But even with that amount of money spent, no one in the industry was certain that it would be possible to eradicate the bug in time to meet the deadline.

The issue was that any big custodian would easily have six hundred vendors with over 3,000 products. It would also have over ninety sub-custodian banks operating in different countries. Testing and monitoring the information from every vendor and sub-custodian bank was a huge and complicated task.

Y2K was a big threat not only to custodians but also to fund-management companies because it might blow up their software systems and put them out of business. Unless software programming was properly fixed, they might not be able to process purchases or liquidations of mutual fund shares or send out client statements, among other problems, in 2000. They also faced double jeopardy: they had to fix their own problems, and they must monitor problems of the custodian banks they used.

At the same time, investors were taking steps to examine whether companies, whose shares their funds owned, had taken appropriate steps so that fund shareholders would not get walloped by Y2K-related stock drops. On the other hand, fund shareholders could wreak havoc themselves by withdrawing huge sums of money thus forcing portfolio managers to sell large blocks of stocks.

While many mutual-fund experts did not expect any significant number of shareholders to take such drastic action, many fund-management firms had arranged credit lines in place to handle share redemptions or a sharp market drop and were prepared to draw on the lines if needed at the year-end.

Many firms were not shy in talking about their preparations, providing details of their Y2K plans on their Web site. But others were reluctant to talk, fearful of revealing information that could be used against them should provisions prove inadequate.

Indeed, not all firms had taken as much action as they could have. The Securities and Exchange Commission required reports on Y2K preparedness from all companies in the US securities industry and took action against seventy-four investment advisors, transfer agents and broker-dealers who neglected to file or filed late.

Freshly coming out of the Asian financial crisis, companies in Asia generally didn't face as much pressure from government regulators to disclose their Y2K plans as US publicly-traded companies did. Preparations for dealing with Y2K problems across the Asia region varied greatly. Some global fund managers were commenting that they wouldn't be surprised by temporary outages and related problems among Asia companies, depending on the sophistication of the country, with China facing the worst setbacks and Hong Kong and Singapore the least.

But Mark Mobius at Templeton Asset Management saw it differently. He argued that emerging-market countries were already accustomed to what in the U.S. would be considered crisis. Electric power outages were par for the course, for example, and thus those countries were ready for such problems and could take them in their stride, he said[17].

17 *Funds Prepare for Y2K Like There's No Tomorrow*, 7 September 1999, *Wall Street Journal*.

Even so, Templeton took other precautionary steps. It asked investors not to cash out or switch their funds until after the New Year. Similarly, it would not offer any new funds in Asia until after 29 February 2000, a leap-year date that also might be troublesome.

In the final months running up to the end of 1999, preparations for Y2K readiness among financial institutions accelerated to the highest tempo. The Global 2000 Coordinating Group, a private-sector organisation comprising more than 240 institutions from fifty-three countries, was leading efforts to ensure readiness of the global financial system. It developed country assessments that attempted to assess the readiness of the financial sector and infrastructure providers such telecommunication, power, water and government. It also published guidelines on contingency-planning and testing activities.

The Custody 2000 Steering Committee, an informal working group within the Global 2000 Coordinating Group comprised thirty-eight of the world's largest custodians, investment banks, regional sub-custodians and international depositories, provided a unified proxy testing environment to ensure sub-custodians' preparedness for the Y2K problem.

Financial regulators around the world also formed The Joint Year 2000 Council to share oversight strategies, approaches and contingency planning, and to serve as a focal point for national and international remediation initiatives.

In March 1999, more than four hundred organisations and five thousand people in the U.S. including major broker-dealers, custodians, stock exchanges, clearing and settlement utilities, vendors, and news providers, representing 98% of the US securities-processing infrastructure, took part in an industry-wide Y2K test under the aegis of the Securities Industry Association (SIA).

Despite the amount of time and resources spent, the industry was cautious about ascertaining that all would be well. 'Based on what we have done, we expect it to be business as usual for individual investors on 3 January', said Margaret Draper of the SIA[18], and: 'We have never issued a definition of compliance or seal of approval, but what I can say is that they have all participated in a thorough testing programme'.

The Paris-based Federation of International Stock Exchanges (FIBV), which represented fifty-four of the world's top bourses and almost all global stock-market capitalisation, said it could not issue a collective clean bill of millennium health.

'Everything you can do internally has been tested on a stand-alone basis, but exchanges are anything but stand-alone as they depend on so many linkages with other things,' said Thomas Krantz, FIBV deputy secretary general[19].

Globally, an estimated US$308 billion was spent among all industries (almost half in the United States) to upgrade computers and application programmes to be Y2K-compliant, according to an IDC (International Data Corporation) report.

Y2K-compliant logo

18 *Y2K – NY Stock Exchange Girds for Possible Trouble*, 12 May 1999, *Reuters*.

19 *Y2K – NY Stock Exchange Girds for Possible Trouble*, 12 May 1999, *Reuters*.

On 31 December 1999, the world held its breath - and nothing happened.

1 January 2000 came in just like any other day. There were no major failures to report anywhere.

'We sat in the data centre eating lasagne and ziti and watched the clock,' recalled a computer analyst in New York. Y2K was a quiet and anti-climactic event.[20]

'As for the midnight switch-over itself, 1999 passed into history with barely a whimper. A few glitches were reported here and there, but nothing catastrophic occurred. The industry would be in crisis soon enough, but as 1 Jan 2000 dawned, nobody saw that one coming yet...' reported CNN[21].

With so much preparation and updated programming done before the change of date, the catastrophe did not happen and only a few, relatively minor, millennium-bug problems occurred.

Countries such as Italy, Russia, and South Korea had done little to prepare for Y2K. They had no more technological problems than those countries, like the U.S., that spent millions of Dollars to combat the problem.

Public relief was soon followed by accusations that the Y2K bug had been greatly exaggerated from the beginning.

Those who had worked in Y2K-compliance efforts insisted that the threat had been real. They maintained that the continued viability of computerised systems was proof that the collective effort had succeeded.

Was the Y2K bug a hoax of the millennium?

---

20 *Y2K: The good, the bad and the crazy*, 28 December 2009, *Computerworld*.

21 *Horror or Hype? Y2K Arrives and World Trembles*, 31 December, 1999, *CNN*.

15. Dot-Com Bubble

Today, it would be very difficult to live our daily lives normally without the Internet. Indeed, the Internet has transformed our lives immensely in many ways, from shopping, to communicating with people, to receiving news, to listening to music.

The Internet has also changed the way business has evolved. Many established businesses and start-ups have made millions off the Internet, and many more are hoping to do the same.

A primitive form of the Internet had been around since 1969, created by government agencies as an efficient way to exchange scientific and military information to computers in different locations. During the mid-1990s, the Internet had evolved as a way for people to communicate via emails, use chat rooms and browse websites.

America Online (AOL) made the Internet available to the general public on a large scale. The Yahoo! search engine and Internet portal was started in 1994 as a directory of websites. The retailer Amazon.com became the first online book retailer and online auction site.

Organisations ranging from corporations to governments rushed in to take advantage of the Internet's power. For the first time in history, mankind could share massive amounts of information at the speed of light using a digital network, a network that offered the potential for mass communication on an unprecedented level. The rise in usage meant an untapped market - an international market.

The tremendous potential of the World Wide Web to transform commerce, communication and the workplace was quickly recognised.

The Internet created a euphoric attitude towards business and inspired much fascination in the future of online commerce. Tech start-ups raced to create the infrastructure and branding necessary to craft massive, far-reaching, digital networks and reach millions and billions of potential customers.

Buzzwords such as 'networking', 'new paradigm', 'information technologies', 'Internet consumer-driven navigation', 'tailored web experience', and many more examples of empty double-speak filled the media.

Many Internet companies, known as 'dot-coms', were launched and investors assumed that a company that operated online was going to be worth millions. From individual dreamers to major corporations, Internet entrepreneurs were basking in dreams of becoming dot-com millionaires or billionaires.

Although some of these new entrepreneurs had realistic plans and business skills, many more of them lacked these attributes but were able to sell their ideas to investors because of the novelty of the dot-com concept and the limitless potential of the Internet.

The initial public offerings (IPO's) of dot-coms emerged with ferocity and frequency, sweeping the world in euphoria. Investors were blindly grabbing every new issue without even looking at a business plan to find out, for example, how long the company would take before making a profit, if ever. Many of these companies' business models relied on aggressively building 'mind-share' by measuring eyeballs (the number of people looking at Web pages) with the expectation that they could build enough brand awareness to charge profitable rates for their services later, even though operating at a sustained net loss in the meanwhile.

Entrepreneur magazine cover on Dot-com; Source: Wikipedia

The dot-com theory went like this: an Internet company's survival depended on expanding its customer base as rapidly as possible even if it produced large annual losses. For instance, Google and Amazon.com did not see any profit in their first years. Amazon was spending to alert people to its existence and expand its customer base, and Google was busy spending to create more powerful machine capacity to serve its expanding search engine. 'Get large or get lost' was the wisdom of the day.

During the loss period, the companies relied on venture capital and IPO's of stocks to pay for their expenses while having no source of income at all. A company's lifespan was measured by its burn rate, i.e. the rate at which the unprofitable company ran through its capital!

It might sound ridiculous but thousands of investors around the world bought the story. These companies raised enormous amounts of money from venture capitalists and other institutional investors. The novelty of these stocks, combined with the difficulty of valuing the companies, sent many stocks to dazzling heights.

A number of online businesses and their founders grew fantastically wealthy. Tech stocks continued to soar and created a very strong incentive for more tech companies to become publicly traded. Many early tech-company shareholders, including employees, became millionaires overnight when their companies went IPO. Tech companies paid their employees in stock options, and the employees profited greatly as long as stocks maintained their strong upward trajectory.

From 1996 to 2000, the NASDAQ stock index exploded from 600 to 5,000 points.

With a low-interest-rate environment and many ordinary people having spare cash for investing, this resulted in a lot of money chasing the new, hyped-up investment opportunities. People quit their jobs to become full-time day-traders.

In the year 1999, there were 457 IPOs in the U.S., most of which were Internet and technology related. Of those 457 IPOs, 117 doubled in price on the first day of trading.

Many dot-com companies were run by people barely out of college and yet were going for million Dollars in market capitalisation. At the peak of the bubble, it was said that a new millionaire was created every sixty seconds in Silicon Valley. Even some tech-company secretaries had option portfolios valued in the millions, while several companies offered BMWs as a sign-on bonus for new employees!

Some analysts started to speculate that we were in a New Economy in which inflation was virtually non-existent and where recessions were a relic of the past. According to this logic, the Old Economy represented traditional bricks-and-mortar businesses, which included sectors such as natural resources and retail stores. Some analysts even believed that corporate earnings and other financial data were not relevant for analysing and investing in technology and Internet-related stocks. Companies would see their stock prices increase by simply adding an e- prefix or a .com to their name.

The Asia region also caught the dot-com fever. In addition to investors pouring money into buying tech stocks listed on the NASDAQ, many Asian dot-com start-ups were also formed in Hong Kong, Singapore, Taiwan, Korea, Japan, and Australia. Most of them were cloning the business model of their counterparts in the Silicon Valley.

In Hong Kong, there were over thirty dot-com IPOs in 1999 and several old-economy companies were reborn as dot-com companies through injection of Internet assets or reverse takeovers.

One of these tech start-ups was Pacific Century Cyberworks (PCCW), formed by Richard Li, son of Hong Kong tycoon Li Ka-Shing. Riding on the dot-com boom, its share price in 2000 reached a high of HK$131.75 and a total market value of HK$41 billion. Through a leveraged financing deal with a syndicated loan co-arranged by Bank of China, Barclays, BNP Paribas and HSBC, it forged Asia's largest-ever corporate takeover at that time and acquired Hong Kong Telecom from its UK Parent, Cable & Wireless, for HK$300 billion in August 2000. Today, PCCW is the largest integrated communications company in Hong Kong, but at the time of the deal, it had only been running for ten months as an Internet investment company and was on its path towards an estimated HK$524 million loss in 2000 before the acquisition.

PCCW Building in Causeway Bay, Hong Kong; source: Wikipedia

The landmark takeover deal saw quite a number of twists and turns. Initially, Cable & Wireless was also considering a bid from Singapore Telecom, chaired by Lee Hsien-Yang, son of Singapore's founding father Lee Kuan-Yew and younger brother of now Prime Minister Lee Hsien-Loong. Lee Hsien-Yang's ambition was supported by media tycoon Rupert Murdoch. But there was local dispute about a Singapore company owning the largest Hong Kong telephone system. Ultimately, PCCW managed to outbid the Singaporean rival.

After the acquisition, Pacific Century Cyberworks Limited changed its English name to PCCW Limited, on 9 August 2002. According to Richard Li, PCCW's future position was to become the world's largest broadband service-provider. In his vision, television programmes and Internet services would be offered to PC users via satellites.

Some other old-economy companies would re-invent themselves by announcing plans to go into Internet businesses to boost their stock prices during the dot-com boom. For example, a property development company, Pearl Oriental Holdings, changed its name into Pearl Oriental Cyberforce and announced plans to move beyond its primary business into provision of Internet-related services, online stock trading, and telecommunications services. During the corporate announcement reception, the Chairman and the executive officers dropped their suits and ties and put on Polo shirts and jeans to project the new Cyber outlook of the reinvented company. Every week would see several similar corporate show-and-tell events.

But, of course, for every company that grew to be a multi-million-Dollar business, hundreds of others failed. A vast number of Internet companies all had the same business plan of monopolising their respective sectors through network effects. Even if the plan was sound, there could only be, at most, one network effects winner in each sector, and therefore most companies with this business plan would fail.

By early 2000, reality started to sink in; investors realised that the dot-com dream had devolved into a classic speculative bubble. The dot-com bubble peaked on 10 March 2000 as the NASDAQ reached at 5,048.62. Then on Monday, 13 March, large numbers of sell orders for major tech stocks such as CISCO and Dell happened to be processed simultaneously and sparked a chain reaction of selling that fed on itself. Within months, the NASDAQ stock index crashed from 5,000 to 2,000. Hundreds of stocks such as Pet.com, which once had a multi-billion Dollar in market capitalisation, were off the map as quickly as they appeared.

In Hong Kong, PCCW's market capitalisation shrank dramatically by 85% in April 2001, from HK$64 billion to HK$8.6 billion. In addition, instead of coming out ahead as a vibrant stock, PCCW stock prices went free fall sagged by a whopping debt of HK$4.2 billion, which eventually exceeded its stock-market value. In 2003, its stock price shed 95%, falling to HK$0.88 from its 2000 peak of HK$28.50.

Globally, panic selling followed while the stock market's value plunged by trillions. By 2002, the NASDAQ stock index plunged to 800. The collapse of these Internet stocks cost investors a whopping US$5 trillion in market value between 2000 and 2002. At the same time, numerous accounting scandals came to light in which tech companies such as WorldCom had artificially inflated their earnings.

Many Internet-based start-ups, communications businesses, and tech firms either lost the vast majority of their share value or went out of business altogether from 2000 to 2005. Hundreds of thousands of tech professionals lost their jobs and, if they had invested in tech stocks, also lost a significant portion of their life savings. Silicon Valley's high-skilled workers were especially impacted. 32% of them were foreign-born and most were from Asia.

The US economy experienced a post dot-com bubble recession, which forced the Federal Reserve to repeatedly cut interest rates from 2001 to stop the bleeding. The New Economy theory was proven wrong and traditional economic principles still held.

During the dot-com boom, Warren Buffett warned that the outsized returns experienced by tech stock investors had dulled them into complacency. After a heady experience of that kind, he said, 'normally sensible people drift into behaviour akin to that of Cinderella at the ball.... They know that overstaying the festivities... will eventually bring on pumpkins and mice'.[22]

But out of the dot-com bubble, a few of these tech companies became absolute game-changers. They were the Google, Amazon, eBay, YouTube, Facebook, Wikipedia, and Twitter of the world. They became essential resources for just about every one of us today.

The shadow of the 2000 dot-com bubble-burst once again looms large because the economy is in another era of huge growth in the tech sector. Alibaba had a history-making US$25 billion IPO on the New York Stock Exchange in September 2014. Companies such as Uber, Palantir and AirBnB are start-ups held privately and worth more than US$1 billion each. While these are e-commerce companies with well-articulated business prospects, what could be worrying is the frenzy with Fintech which has been attracting billions of investment for their novel, disruptive ideas even though many of them do not have a business plan.

Are we in an Internet bubble 2.0 or 3.0?

Or is it, as many analysts would say, 'this time is different'?

22 *Warren Buffet: 'I told you so'*, 13 March, 2001, *BBC News*

16. September 11

It was a normal day in Hong Kong on Tuesday, 11 September 2001. I left the office after finishing a conference call on the launch of the first open-ended fund in China, picked up my wife from work in Central and took a taxi home at around 8:30pm. On the way, I started receiving emails on my Blackberry from colleagues in Chicago that something unusual was happening in New York. They were not sure what it was.

When I got home and turned on the TV, images of the Two World Trade Center struck by the United Airlines airplane and soon bursting into flames were broadcast on air repeatedly again and again. A horrifying event had happened. It was a terrorist attack!

World Trade Center Tower in flames; Source: Wikipedia

Even today, years afterwards, these images are still broadcast around the world every now and then, reminding us of the horrifying event.

September 11 has undoubtedly made the most lasting social, economic and political impact on the United States and world since the turn of the century.

The destruction of the World Trade Center and nearby infrastructure caused calamitous damage to the economy of Lower Manhattan and had a significant effect on the global financial markets, closing Wall Street for six days until September 17. It caused havoc to the banking world globally.

To custodians, it was a humbling experience, testing our ability to maintain continuous operation with black-swan events.

In the U.S., only a handful of custodian banks processed most of the securities and cash flowing through the financial markets. It had been taken for granted that these banks would have sound business-continuity plans at the ready to manage extreme situations. But September 11 showed that custodian banks could be the Achilles heel of the global financial-services industry.

The World Trade Center housed several wholesale brokers and large trading operations that played essential roles in the financial markets. In addition, several of these firms, such as Cantor Fitzgerald, suffered devastating losses of employees. The communications network and the primary operations of many payment-services providers near the World Trade Center were disrupted as fire, debris, and water destroyed or damaged much of the power, telecommunications and transportation infrastructure serving lower Manhattan's financial district. Workers in the vicinity of the World Trade Center were forced to evacuate their buildings immediately after the attacks occurred.

The custodian bank at the epicentre of this disastrous event was The Bank of New York (BONY).

Before September 11, BONY's primary business locations were in Lower Manhattan, including:

- One Wall Street - Corporate Headquarters
- 32 Old Slip - FX, Securities Lending, Treasury Operations
- 101 Barclay Street - Funds Transfers, Stock Transfers, Depositary Receipts, Corporate Trust, Broker Dealer Services
- 100 Church Street - Fund Accounting, Mutual Fund Custody

All four locations were within walking distance of the World Trade Center.[23]

After the terrorist attacks on the World Trade Center on September 11, BONY had to evacuate 8,300 staff from these locations and implement its contingency plans. 101 Barclay Street and 100 Church Street were most impacted due to their proximity to the World Trade Center. Processing had to be distributed to recovery centres in New Jersey and sites in other parts of New York. Corporate Headquarters was moved from One Wall Street to 1290 Sixth Avenue.

However, telecommunications outages delayed the recovery process and personnel had difficulty reaching recovery centres. Client connectivity to BONY's critical systems, such as the Government Securities Clearing System and collateral management systems, were interrupted. Communications between BONY and the Federal Reserve

23 *The Bank of New York Mellon and the Impact of September 11, 2001*, presentation by Paul Bodart, March 2011.

and DTC (Depository Trust Company) were interrupted. Connectivity among BONY's systems located in different sites was interrupted.

The processing and communications disruptions suffered by BONY on September 11 left many banks, investment managers, brokers and financial-services firms unsure about the status of their transactions and others waiting for cash that had been promised to counter-parties.

As a result, large imbalances, especially in government securities settlement, had developed. Transaction values on Fedwire fell 24% below their normal level compared with the August average. The imbalances were extraordinarily large, and the ability of individual financial institutions to work around operational difficulties or to tap alternative sources of liquidity was highly constrained.

It became apparent just how interconnected the financial-services industry is and how custodian banks sit at the nexus of that web. The Fed took quick action by keeping the discount window open for loans, and also used open-market operations to inject massive amounts of liquidity into the market to keep the wheels greased and rolling.

The Fedwire and CHIPS payment systems operated throughout September 11 and on the following days because most of their operations were not located in downtown New York. The clearing and settlement system for US government securities laboured under severe difficulties due to the disruptions at BONY, but trading in government securities was able to resume on 13 September. Redemptions and rollovers of commercial paper were temporarily disrupted, but equities trades made in the days just before September 11 were fully processed and settled. On 17 September, when the major U.S. stock exchanges reopened, payments and securities settlements successfully completed processing the largest volume of trading that had ever occurred in a single day in New York Stock Exchange history.

The September 11 events put the business contingency plans of custodian banks and the financial industry to unprecedented tests and challenges for an extended period. Lessons learned from the disaster resulted in many new ideas and operating models that have significantly changed the industry's business-continuity planning practices today to ensure operational resilience of the financial system.

One of the main lessons learned from the BONY experience is the importance of having data centres geographically dispersed.

In fact, after September 11, BONY did not re-occupy all its former downtown locations. It took 1.2 million square feet of office space in midtown Manhattan to re-establish the data centres it previously maintained at 101 Barclay and 100 Church. While the basic structure of its business-continuity plan was not significantly changed, the locations were changed so that BONY now has its staff much more spread apart.

Then there was the question of the business-continuity model. JP Morgan Chase's Treasury Services division moved into a new 150,000 square foot site in Tampa, Florida with a back-up facility in Orlando sixty miles away.[24] The Orlando facility was to become a hot site - a disaster-recovery site stocked with all the equipment needed to continue operations such as office space and furniture, telephone jacks and computer equipment - as opposed to cold sites used by many firms previously that simply consisted of office space and took a long time to become operational.

But September 11 also showed just how difficult it is to have a back-up installation far away enough to be on a different electric power grid or beyond the reach of the same natural disaster such as an

24 *BCP & the Custodian Bank*, 1 July 2002, *wallstreetandtech.com*

earthquake, hurricane, flood, etc., and yet close enough to be reached quickly. In a move almost no one had thought possible, September 11 saw New York City locked down, leaving employees unable to reach their back-up sites in New Jersey and Brooklyn for most of the day.

Northern Trust, with its Chicago and London operations running off the same platform, operated those two sites to function as each other's back-up locations during September 11. Since the event, it further developed its contingency plan on inter-country back-up of its operations hubs rather than keeping expensive hot sites waiting across town or across the country, which employees might never get to.

In addition, the September 11 attacks showed that giving employees the technology to work from the only place they want to be during a crisis - home - may be the best long-term solution for custodian banks. Northern Trust worked with Citrix, a vendor of application-server and portal products, to develop a virtual-private network or VPN so employees could access the company's applications securely from home.

The critical role of telecommunications in business-continuity planning was also highlighted by the disaster. Many firms that were nowhere near the World Trade Center nonetheless suffered from damage caused to the area's telecommunications switching stations. Some, who were connected with multiple carriers to secure operational redundancy, found that lines from different telecommunications companies followed the same routing. Having a complete end-to-end route of the mission-critical circuits would help them to improvise depending on the actual situation.

With regard to the development of a business-continuity plan, one of the most important aspects is to get the technology, business and contingency-planning leaders to work together to hash out what needs to be done, what is expected during a crisis, and what is technologically feasible. It is no longer a task that can be left to operations to handle alone.

The other key aspect is testing the plan under myriad scenarios to make sure it works. When something happens for real, you don't have time to have conversations, you just have to mobilise the teams and start executing the plan immediately.

Finally, the events of September 11 demonstrated that business-continuity plans, procedures and testing need to reflect internal interdependencies, such as between payments, custody, funding, trading, and issuing/paying agency functions, as well as external dependencies and relationships. In addition to operational and safety decisions, financial institutions need to make credit and market risk judgments with respect to customers and counterparties, whose financial condition may not be certain during a crisis.

Regulators in matured financial centres, such as Singapore, have since 2001 annually held industry-wide coordinated testing of business-continuity plans between institutions and their customers or counter-parties as an industry practice.

Among the many review reports about September 11, an IMF publication commented: 'Contingency planning advanced substantially in the run-up to the century date change (Y2K). Y2K planning incorporated the involvement of senior management and boards of directors and asked business managers to consider how they would operate their businesses, and not just their back offices, in the event of a Y2K-related disruption....... federal bank regulators noted that detailed contingency plans developed for Y2K specified the minimum level of output and services necessary for each major business process. They also noted that simulated operational failures and scenario building helped reduce the time needed to respond to operational problems and improved decision making and internal communication......'[25]

Had the financial industry not invested millions of Dollars of investment in Y2K planning several years earlier, would September 11 have had an even more crippling impact on the industry?

25 *September 11 and the U.S. Payment System*, March 2002, *Finance & Development* (A quarterly IMF publication)

17. First Open-Ended Fund

Globally, 2001 was remembered for the dot-com bubble burst and the September 11 attack in the U.S.

For China, 2001 marked the year of a new era in its fund-management industry in addition to its high-profile accession to the World Trade Organisation after fifteen years of negotiation.

The capital market in China, as we know it today, started just more than twenty-five years ago, much later than many of the other Asian countries. The current Shanghai Stock Exchange was re-established on 26 November 1990 and began operation on 19 December after an interruption of forty-one years. During the first year, only fifteen companies made a debut listing on the stock exchange with a total market cap of RMB10.9 billion.

It did not take much time, however, for people in China to accept stock investment. By 2000, the total market cap jumped to RMB4,774 billion with close to 1,100 companies listed on the Shanghai and Shenzhen exchanges. While it was only 18.27% of the total market cap of the Tokyo Stock Exchange and was also lower than that of Hong Kong, it was already higher than Taiwan, Korea or Singapore.

The fund-management industry formally started after *Interim Measures for the Management of Securities Investment Funds* was published on 14 November 1997. On 27 March 1998, China Southern Fund Management and Guotai Fund Management launched the first two closed-ended funds, each of RMB2 billion in asset value. By June 2000, the industry had grown to ten fund-management companies and twenty-two closed-ended funds with a total of RMB50.5 billion in assets under management. The SHSE Fund Index was introduced to capture the performance of regulated closed-ended funds listed on the Exchange to reflect changes in China's growing securities investment fund market.

Meanwhile, China's GDP was growing double-digit annually. According to the IMF, the GDP per capital in 2000 was US$951, an increase that made it three times the level of a decade earlier. National gross savings was 37.3% of the GDP or US$450.9 billion (about RMB6 trillion), of which two thirds were household savings. Time was ripe to introduce open-ended funds for the mass population to transfer savings into investment by fund-management professionals and to add liquidity to the domestic stock market.

In October 2000, the China Securities Regulatory Commission (CSRC) issued *Provisional Rules for Open-Ended Funds*, allowing open-ended funds to be set up with a minimum of one hundred investors per fund and RMB200 million in fund size. In addition, it allowed the commission fee of an open-ended fund to be charged at up to 5% of the purchase price during subscription, and at up to 3% of the sales price during redemption.

The whole market was full of excitement about this new product initiative.

However, the CSRC was concerned with the level of expertise and experience of the local fund-management companies and custodian banks in managing and administering these funds that were primarily aimed at retail investors. It came up with an idea that domestic fund-management companies needed to have a foreign partner as a technical adviser for managing these open-ended funds. Similarly, custodian banks need to find a world-renowned foreign custodian in advising them on administering these funds. This would be a key criterion in the overall assessment of their qualification to become an investment manager or custodian for these new funds. This triggered a rush for strategic alliances by both Chinese domestic fund-management companies and custodian banks.

The next several months saw a number of tie-ups (dubbed marriages of convenience[26] by *Pensions Asia*) quickly formed between Chinese and foreign custodians:

- Agricultural Bank of China with Bank of New York
- Bank of China with Deutsche Bank
- Bank of Communications with JP Morgan
- China Construction Bank with JP Morgan
- Industrial and Commercial Bank of China with State Street

One of my business goals at Northern Trust was to bring the bank to the China market as the next step of development after Hong Kong and Singapore where the bank had already established a presence. Prior to this, Northern Trust had no contacts with China; it was an unknown name in the market. The Chinese custodians were looking for brand names to sign cooperation agreements with and Northern Trust was not on their shopping list.

Then an opportunity came up. Through an introduction, I met Bank of Communications' (BoComm) head of Asset Custody Department, Mr. Xie Hong-Bing, in Shanghai in October 2000. BoComm had signed a Memorandum of Understanding (MOU) less than two months ago with JP Morgan for cooperation in the custody business.

---

26 *Marriages of convenience*, April 2001, *PensionsAsia*.

However, several weeks later, JP Morgan signed a similar MOU with China Construction Bank. This opportunistic approach did not please BoComm who saw it as somehow disloyal.

We had a very open and positive discussion. Mr. Xie made it very clear that they wanted to find a partner truly committed to teaching and helping BoComm to build its custody business in China. Like the other custodian banks, they had been partnering with fund-management companies to launch an open-ended fund. Their client was Huaan Fund Management, which had been established in 1998 by Shanghai Investment Trust and four other securities companies. JP Morgan Fleming Asset Management was their technical advisor on the fund launch. BoComm needed help to build up their know-how quickly.

The exchanges and discussions that ensued went very positively. Relative to the other competitors, both banks were smaller and were more eager to seize the new business opportunities in China. Both banks had a very down-to-earth culture and worked with each other as equal partners. There was perfect compatibility.

In May 2001, Mr. Xie and two other senior members of his department travelled with me to Chicago to spend a week learning more about how custody and fund administration worked and the relationship was further strengthened and institutionalised. After the trip, the open-ended fund project went full speed. We provided a series of training sessions to the BoComm team and technical support to help them prepare for their CSRC application and to set up operational procedures for processing and supporting open-ended funds.

Huaan's Innovation Investment Fund emerged as the front-runner for approval by CSRC as the first open-ended fund among the six applications received from Chinese fund-management companies. The fund would be investing in Chinese companies that used innovative technology and management - about 80% in A-Shares and 20% in domestic bonds. The fund size would be capped at an initial value of RMB5 billion, and would be sold to both Chinese retail and institutional investors - 60% made available to individuals and 40% to institutions. BoComm would be the custodian.

Northern Trust's President of Corporate & Institutional Services,
Mr. Peter Rossiter, signed cooperation agreement with Bank of Communications' Deputy Director-General, Mr. Li Jun.
Source: Author's photo collection

In the run-up to the fund launch, days and nights were spent on working out the details of operational flows and procedures and in testing the system, but there was one critical issue to resolve: how to manage the sales process and fund subscriptions?

At this nascent stage of China's stock-market development, many people were naively attracted by the prospect of the rise of stock prices and saw securities investment as an opportunity to get rich quickly. A number of stock IPOs attracted hundreds of thousands of people lining up at bank branches for subscription and minor riots erupted due to crowd misbehaviour.

The biggest concern was not that the Huaan fund would not sell, but that it would be at least several times oversubscribed given the buoyant investor sentiment in the domestic stock market, and thus would attract billions of Yuans' worth of investment capital. It was critical to look at ways to cope with the expected overwhelming demand, in order to ensure that the offering would be orderly and the potential impact on social stability would not be undermined.

Several different options, including a lottery draw, were discussed to establish the best and fairest allocation method for the expected over-subscription without creating social instability. After much deliberation between all the parties in consultation with CSRC, it was ultimately decided that the fund would still be sold directly but only through 139 of BoComm's banking outlets in thirteen major cities instead of throughout the country like previous stock IPO's. The threshold for individual investors to bid for the new open-ended fund was set at RMB10,000 with a maximum limit of RMB300,000. Redemption within the first three months was not allowed.

On 11 September 2001 – hours before the World Trade Center terrorist attack as Asia is ahead in time zone - the fund was launched. Domestic investors flocked to subscribe to China's first-ever offering of open-ended mutual funds. In the first two hours, investors snapped up half of the 3 billion Yuan open-ended mutual funds allotted for retail investors.

'Each outlet received an average of more than 10 million Yuan in subscriptions within two hours this morning,' reported *South China Morning Post* quoting a source close to Huaan Fund Management[27].

Investors lined up at sales outlets from early morning; Source: news.sohu.com

China News Agency reported that a seventy-year-old Beijing retiree, who had never invested in the stock market, travelled all the way to Fuzhou and lined up for seventeen hours before he successfully bought subscription of the fund.

27 *First open-ended fund offering popular*, 11 September 2001, *South China Morning Post*.

Mr. Zhao surrounded by reporters after successfully bought the fund;
Source: news.sohu.com

By noon, more than 90% of the retail allocation had been subscribed. There was no major commotion or incident reported at any of the sales outlets.

The first open-ended fund in China was born.

18. The Outbreak

It was like a chapter taken out of Albert Camus's existentialist novel *The Plague*. Hong Kong was like a ghost town. Shopping malls, restaurants and cinemas were deserted. A whole apartment complex at Amoy Gardens in Kowloon Bay was quarantined. Schools were temporarily closed. The people lurching around in the streets were all wearing face masks and avoided close contacts with each other. People who became sick with symptoms of a previously unknown virus were put into isolation for ten days for observation and treatment. Hospitals were over-run. The economy ground to a halt. There was much fear in the air.

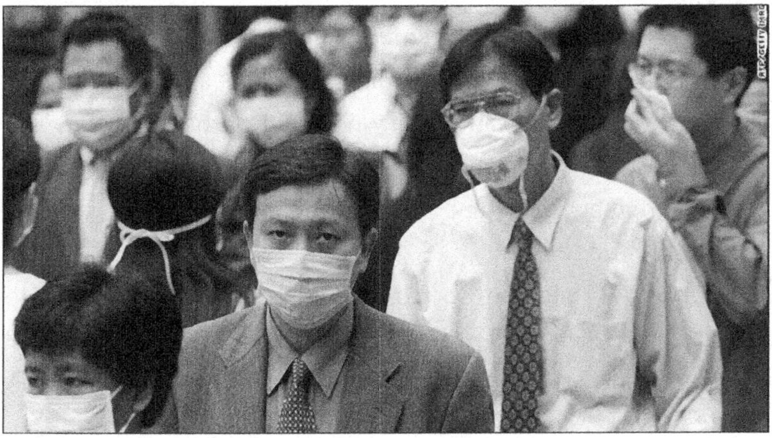

Hong Kong people in surgical masks in public areas;
Source: smh.com.au

That was March 2003. The World Health Organisation (WHO) issued a global alert based on an ominous warning of a worldwide health threat due the outbreak of an unknown form of severe pneumonia called SARS (Severe Acute Respiratory Syndrome), which was contagious and deadly. Hong Kong was hit hard by the virus and became a city under siege.

The virus first appeared in China's southern Guangdong province in November 2002. It spread to Hong Kong from a mainland doctor who arrived in February 2003 and stayed at the ninth floor of the Metropole Hotel in Kowloon, infecting sixteen other hotel visitors. Those visitors then travelled to Canada, Singapore, Taiwan, and Vietnam, spreading SARS to those countries as well as a result.

SARS was a serious threat to businesses, not only in terms of financial impact on the bottom-line but also in maintaining continuity of operation.

Over the past few years, businesses had spent a lot of money and resources on preparing back-up plans for the much anticipated Y2K computer problems that were once expected to wreak havoc. Then the black-swan events of September 11 in 2001 pushed those same businesses into doomsday preparations. But the arrival of the SARS virus proved to be yet an entirely new test of the unknown. The spotlight was very much on human beings as a critical component of any comprehensive strategy for operational resilience.

As cases of SARS infections soared and the number of deaths started to increase, international and local companies across Asia attempted to put in place new measures to ensure that their operations could continue.

Like other businesses, banks and custodians were confronted with the key challenge: how to safeguard staff's health while preparing for possible disruption of operations. Previous business-continuity plans had assumed implicitly that some staff would always be available to maintain operations in the event of a major operational disruption; SARS made it clear that this assumption was not valid.

Northern Trust had just over fifty staff in total between the two offices in Hong Kong and Singapore at this time. We formed a small central-command unit comprised of myself and several other senior managers to discuss and decide each morning what measures to take upon the latest information we obtained about the epidemic.

As SARS was basically an unknown virus even to the medical professionals, we had to improvise and to deal with the situation as it occurred. Based on guidelines from the Hong Kong and Singapore government and the Hong Kong Monetary Authority and the Monetary Authority of Singapore, we implemented a number of measures to maintain a high level of environmental hygiene in the office.

First of all, all staff were required to have influenza vaccinations - for individual protection and to reduce the number of false alarms and disruptions. A compulsory routine was enforced for all staff coming into office in the morning, to self-take body temperature with results recorded in a roster. Anybody with flu or a higher body temperature than normal would be asked to leave and stay home.

Temperature taking routine in school; Source: www.eco-business.com

A casual dress code was introduced to facilitate the cleaning and disinfecting of clothing. Staff who were pregnant were asked to take early maternity leave. Face masks were distributed and we all had to wear them inside the office at all times. All objects that were subject to frequent public contacts, such as hand rails, door knobs, lift buttons, telephones, etc., were disinfected every hour throughout the day.

A small conference room somewhat separated from the rest of the office was identified to become the emergency isolation room should any staff show symptoms of the virus during office hours.

Face-to-face contact with customers or external parties was discouraged in favour of telephone and other electronic means such as web- or video-conferencing. Travelling to another country especially to a SARS-affected location required exceptional approval.

Protocols were established for communicating daily to Chicago head-office on the latest situations and developments, and to the authorities should there be any suspected case of infection, and for sending home colleagues in contact with infected staff members.

Some bigger banking institutions started to operate in a split-operation mode by basing their critical business teams in both their main site and their back-up facilities, so that, should the emergency situation of a massive quarantine occur, they could still continue operating with the capacity and the necessary staff at the unaffected site. In other organisations, redundancy was introduced by moving parts of their teams to separate overseas office locations for the duration of the outbreak.

With a relatively small work force in our two offices, we had no choice but run one single operation despite the risk. We had cross-border back-up plans in place between Hong Kong and Singapore but, obviously, that was not of much use since both Hong Kong and Singapore were hit by SARS at the same time. We had to make arrangements with offices in London and Chicago to cover the critical activities of cash and trade processing and settlement, and foreign-exchange dealing in case our offices in Hong Kong or Singapore were not operational.

However, the risk of SARS to staff was not just at the place of work but from the time that they left their homes to get on the subway or public buses. By the time they got to the office they might well have been exposed already.

We had a scare of a suspected infection case in the Singapore office. A female member of staff felt sick during the day in the office and went to see the doctor. The next day, it was reported in the news that a patient who went to that same clinic the previous day was suspected to be infected with SARS and the whole clinic including the doctor and the nurses had had to be quarantined. We were shocked to hear this news and were wondering whether we should organise a mass quarantine and whether we should all work from home. Ultimately, it was found that our staff and the infected carrier went to the clinic at different times of the day. They missed each other by just over an hour!

Supplies of face masks became another issue because they were running out very quickly in both Hong Kong and Singapore. But fortunately, being a subsidiary of a multinational firm, we were able to get supplies shipped over from Chicago – a tangible form of support in addition to the moral support that we had been receiving throughout the crisis.

I was personally caught in the logistics of the precaution measures because I had just moved to Singapore at this time to assume the role of head of the region while my family stayed in Hong Kong until summer for my daughters to finish their school term; each time I went back to Hong Kong, I had to stay in self quarantine for ten days before physically going back to the Singapore office. But the work-from-home VPN technology that had been implemented at the bank since September 11 proved to be very useful and allowed me to fulfil both my professional and family duties without major disruption other than the mental strain and emotional anxiety involved in the process.

As each day passed, new cases of SARS infection were discovered and the sense of fear and uncertainty continued to grow.

The economic and political backdrop to the disease didn't help. The WHO announcement came just days before the 2003 Iraq War began. The September 11 terrorist attacks were still fresh in the public psyche, and before the disease was identified many serious questions were being asked as to whether it was bio-terrorism attack.

There was a general, uneasy emotional backdrop. 'Life is not safe, the world is not safe, even the ground under my feet I can't count on,' a local counsellor commented. 'People are very, very tired and very insecure.'[28]

But as weeks passed, people started to adapt social conventions and the epidemic became part of daily life: a public service announcement suggested Japanese-like bows rather than handshakes at business meetings; signs offered instruction on how to wash hands and on proper spitting etiquette; money changing hands suddenly took on new scrutiny; catholic priests were forbidden from offering sacramental wine and placing communion wafers in the mouths of the faithful.[29]

---

28 *Hong Kong and SARS: A city under siege*, 21 February 2013, *CNN*.

29 *Hong Kong and SARS: A city under siege*, 21 February 2013, *CNN*.

It was reported that people turned masks into fashion statements, embroidering their surgical masks with personalised decorations. Other entrepreneurs started selling masks with Hello Kitty or other cartoon characters. LVMH Moët Hennessy Louis Vuitton, for its part, was annoyed by photos showing Hong Kong residents, wearing face masks to protect from SARS that bore counterfeit Louis Vuitton logos, that appeared in European fashion magazines such as Elle. [30]

The SARS outbreak officially ended on 23 June 2003 when the WHO removed Hong Kong from the list of affected countries. It resulted in 1,755 cases of infection and three hundred deaths in Hong Kong. Singapore reported more than thirty deaths. Overall, it had spread to twenty-nine countries and three regions, with a cumulative total of 8,422 cases of infection and 916 deaths.

The macroeconomic impact of SARS on the region was estimated to stand at anything up to US$100 billion in 2003 prices. Across Asia, growth rates were reduced by SARS by between one to four percentage points. Three areas of these economies had been particularly vulnerable to the SARS outbreak: retail consumption, tourism, and re-exports.

Nonetheless, the SARS outbreak had also created positive legacy. Besides enhancing the depth of business-continuity plans to include infectious epidemics and the wide use of electronic communications in these plans, the SARS outbreak also had a profound effect on Internet usages:

'....from late March through to May...traffic to Internet sites from shopping, banking, news, medical information and education grew to record highs,' reported Nielsen/Net Ratings Hong Kong. While Internet

30 *Economies hurt by SARS and Fear*, 21 April 2003, *The New York Times.*

usage declined slightly post-SARS following peak levels during the outbreak, our June figures still show significant increases over February.... 'There is little doubt that Internet audiences post-SARS have reached significantly higher levels than before the epidemic.'[31]

This increased use of the Internet paved the way for investments in the Internet and growth of its usage in banking and other businesses in the following years.

31 *SARS stimulates ongoing growth in Internet Usage in Hong Kong*, 1 August 2003, *intelligentasia.com*

19. Social Security System

When the economic growth in the Asia region started to slow down quickly from double or high-single digit in the late 1990's, one fact became painfully apparent: most countries had not developed sound pension systems to supplement traditional support mechanisms for taking care of their elderly in face of an ageing population.

The result was a mad rush for pension reforms in the following decade.

Apart from tweaking existing structures, many countries attempted to adopt the three-pillar model published in the World Bank's 1994 report *Averting the Old-Age Crisis: Policies to Protect the Old and Promote Growth* for creating sustainable, sensible and broad-based pension systems, namely:

- Pillar 1 - A standardised, state-run pension system, which offers basic coverage and is primarily focused on reducing poverty.
- Pillar 2 - A funded system that recipients and employers pay into including defined benefit pension funds and defined contribution accounts/plans.
- Pillar 3 - Voluntary private funded accounts, including individual saving plans, insurance, etc.

Countries across the region introduced a number of key initiatives during the 2000's to catch up:

- Hong Kong – Mandatory Pension Fund (2000).
- China – National Social Security Fund (2000), Enterprise Annuity voluntary plans (2004).

- Singapore – Supplementary Retirement Scheme (2001).
- New Zealand – New Zealand Superannuation Fund (2001), KiwiSaver voluntary savings scheme (2007).
- Japan – Defined benefit (2001) and defined contribution (2002) Employee Pension Schemes, National Pension Fund Association for the self-employed (2004).
- India - New Pension System defined contribution plans (2004).
- Korea – Employee Retirement Security voluntary defined benefit or defined contribution plans (2005).
- Taiwan – New Labour Pension Scheme defined-contribution individual retirement accounts (2005).

It was the decade of pension reforms in Asia.

Most of these initiatives became key pillars for the pension systems in place today in these countries. They created a stream of new business opportunities for fund managers as well as for custodians as these new pension funds started gathering contributions. Collectively, they provided a strong boost to the growth of the fund-management and custody industry across the region.

But among these initiatives, China made the most far-reaching structural reforms in its pension system.

Traditionally, China's retirement benefits were handled by state-owned enterprises (SOE) on a pay-as-you-go basis, where the younger generation supports the older generation. Besides health care, SOEs would take care of their employees when they retired at the age of sixty for men and fifty-five for women with very high payouts. This was part of the iron rice-bowl of the socialist system, being an integral part of the all-encompassing social welfare for employees of the SOEs. However, the system did not work. Not only did the structure make it difficult to offer such generous benefits but also it was based on the solvency of the SOEs. And when a SOE went bankrupt, so did its unfunded pension benefits.

China was not exempt from negative demographic developments. According to several studies in the late 1990's, the working population as a proportion of the total population was forecast to peak in 2010 and then fall steadily afterwards. The median age would rise from 32.5 years in 2005 to 48 years in 2050. Since 1979, most people in China had been limited to having one child. As a result, there were not enough young people to take care of the elderly, either directly or indirectly, through government tax revenues or a pay-as-you-go (PAYG) plan. The one-child policy had created the 1-2-4 problem, in which one person in the work force had to take care of two parents and four grandparents.

The ageing population of China; Source: www.gdszzm.com

The Chinese government did take the issue of ageing population seriously, not only in the interest of protecting its citizens for life but also for fear that it would cause social instability – the euphemism for sit-ins, demonstrations and protests which regularly happened around the country during the SOE restructuring reforms in the 1990's.

In 1997, the State Council decided to embark on comprehensive social-security reforms with the promulgation of Document No. 26, which laid out the conceptual framework for a multi-pillared system to replace the pay-as-you-go scheme. A new social-security system was created. The first pillar would be a basic mandatory PAYG pension scheme to be financed by the government; the second pillar would be an individual account funded by mandatory employer and employee contributions; the third pillar would be a voluntary account also funded by the employer and employee.

Although the central government had dictated the direction of pension reform, it left the implementation to provincial governments, labour and social-security bureaus. The transition had mixed results. Wealthier coastal cities and provinces had greater success in developing the second and third pillars, but the poorer provinces had difficulty with their pension reforms due to a lack of money. Although individual accounts were set up for every Chinese employee who had been working, retirees were still drawing a pension under the PAYG system. With bankrupt state-owned enterprises unable to pay contributions to fund the PAYG system, many poorer provinces took the money that was supposed to be in the individual accounts of the present workers to pay for the pension of today's retirees. This resulted in massive numbers of unfunded accounts.

By end of 2000, the size of unfunded individual accounts reached RMB199 billion (US$24.3 billion). There was very high probability that the individual accounts would not be able to meet their obligations. In addition, the diversion of funds from individual accounts undermined the objective of establishing the multi-pillared system, and that in turn undermined public's confidence in the government's resolve to introduce a fully-funded pension scheme, and reduced their incentives to contribute to the new pension accounts.

To address the problem, the Central Committee of CPC (Communist Party of China) and the State Council decided on 1 August 2000 to establish the National Social Security Fund (NSSF), and set up the National Council for Social Security Fund (NaCSSF) for managing and operating the NSSF's assets. The NSSF aimed to serve as a strategic reserve fund of last resort at the central government level to support future social-security expenditures and liability gaps.

The assets of the NSSF would come from four sources:

- Fiscal transfers from the central government budget.
- Proceeds from the listing of state-owned enterprises.
- Lottery proceeds.
- Investment income.

The NaCSSF's mandate was to enhance the value of the fund's assets with prudent management. Over time, the NSSF would likely become the largest pension fund in Asia. The Chinese government estimated that in the next ten years the NaCSSF would become an agency that would have US$120 billion under its administration. In 2002, China's stock market capitalisation was a little more than US$500 billion, the second largest in Asia. Thus, the NSSF would be a significant institutional investor and would play a critical role in shaping the development of China's capital markets.

Obviously, the challenge was humongous. A fund of such magnitude would have to be very well managed and would need capabilities beyond the expertise and experience of the fledging fund-management industry in China at that time. It would have to draw on expertise from the developed countries. The NaCSSF decided to look to foreign expertise for assistance similar to the CSRC's approach in launching Chinese open-ended funds.

The call for assistance met with a very positive response from the international donor community.

In November 2001, the Asian Development Bank (ADB) announced an offering to China of a US$1 million technical-assistance (TA) grant to help reform the mainland's pension system. Of that grant, US$400,000 was allocated to employ a consultant for the NaCSSF to set up asset allocation models and investment guidelines as well as selecting investment managers. The remaining US$600,000 of the grant was slated for hiring a consultant to assist in the pilot pension-reform scheme in Liaoning province.

Liaoning province, in China's rust belt, had had the most problems with pension reforms and Premier Zhu Rong-Ji decided to implement the trial reforms in Liaoning after visiting the province in 1999 and seeing first-hand how pension debt was preventing state-owned enterprises from restructuring. Unlike previous pension reforms handled by local governments, the Liaoning pilot project was overseen by the central government. The main feature of Liaoning's pilot project was to separate the pooling from the individual accounts. Under the trial project, retirees no longer received pensions from their former enterprises and would get their money from the municipal social-security office.

ADB's technical assistance grant would allow the Liaoning pilot project to hire a consultant to build forecast models to enable the government to do more financial planning, strengthen the social-security departments in the province, and set up an information-technology system to complete the bookkeeping.

In July 2002, ADB announced that Hewitt Associates, a global management consulting firm headed by Steward Leckie in Asia, was selected for the mandate to help the pilot project in Liaoning province, and *Caisse de Depot et Placement du Quebec* (CDP), a Canadian fund manager, for the mandate to help the NaCSSF.

While the ADB grant attracted most of the limelight, another international body was also making a more low-key support effort for the newly set up NSSF in China. At the beginning of 2001, it came to the notice of a colleague of mine based in Chicago, Kevin Tan, that the World Bank was also discussing with NaCSSF about providing technical assistance to help them set up the middle- and back-office functions to supplement ADB's TA project to help them set up the front office functions. The project would focus on one critical element of the NSSF - risk control and management. This would assist the NSSF in establishing appropriate risk-management processes for the prudent investment of assets.

This would very much fall into the subject expertise of a global custodian with a strong base of pension-fund clients in the U.S. and other countries. Kevin and I approached Northern Trust's management and gained the support of Steve Fradkin, then Global Head of Sales - Corporate and Institutional Services, to make a proposal to the World Bank to bid for the consultancy mandate. The two of us would be the lead consultants for the project.

It turned out that we were the only custodian bank bidding for the mandate. We were short-listed alongside with another global consulting firm for the selection interview with the NaCSSF. As in the case of selecting CDP for the ADB mandate, NaCSSF ultimately preferred partnering with an industry practitioner and we demonstrated actual experience and expertise that we could share with them based on Northern Trust's own treasury investment operations as well as the broad base of client portfolio investments that we supported in these areas. We were ultimately selected.

The NSSF team led by Mr. Wang Wen-Ling, Director – Legal & Compliance, (middle) at work on the project with Northern Trust consultants (Lawrence Au, third from right, and Kevin Tan, second from right); Source: Author's photo collection

In November 2002, Northern Trust signed the contract for the technical assistance project with International Financial Corporation (IFC), a World Bank subsidiary. The comprehensive project was scheduled to take nine months to complete. Guided by the IFC, we would provide assistance to the NaCSSF in their internal risk-management control processes and systems, including: asset allocation process, investment management monitoring process, investment performance measurement process, and portfolio risk and returns assessment and optimisation process.

The NaCSSF had just over thirty staff at that time, with about RMB124 billion under its management. It was a freshly formed organisation, with Mr. Xiang Huai-Cheng, a former Finance Minister, as Chairman and Mr. Gao Xi-Qing, former vice chairman of CSRC, as his deputy. The senior management team members came from all sorts of backgrounds and only a few were from banking and finance. The working levels were the *crème de la crème* of the country, joining the organisation through open recruitment. At any discussion meeting during the project, we had never in our lives had so many PHD's in the room with us. There was a strong sense of mission in the organisation - to create a legacy for the country that would be making an impact on the welfare of 1.3 billion people for generations.

We started the TA project in December 2002 and completed it in May 2004, eight months longer than scheduled because of travel restrictions during the first half of 2002 due to the SARS outbreak in China. The project was structured in three phases, with recommendations proposed at the end of each phase. A total of seventy-eight specific recommendations were made during the three phases of the whole project. Of these, fourteen of them were implemented by the end of April 2004, and another fifty-nine of them were in the process of implementation over the next twelve months. Both the IFC and NaCSSF were very complimentary about the outcome of the project and the practicality of the recommendations for implementation.

In the course of conducting the first TA, it became evident that NaCSSF would also benefit from the experience of the consultancy to draw on the best practices of other global investment organisations to establish policies and procedures in its Finance and Accounting Department responsible for managing external managers and custodians and for monitoring their service, and to develop back-up and contingency plans in its IT Department. The IFC agreed to provide a second grant. The second TA started right after the first and was completed in June 2005.

The two TA projects spanning two-and-a-half years in total were a fascinating experience. Being the best and the brightest in the country, the NSSF staff were very intelligent and knowledgeable about the subject matter of investment operations and risk management in theory. Where we were able to add significant value in the projects was by bringing in the actual experience of other international institutions, and in suggesting the ways in which their theories could be translated to practical use within their organisation.

The Chinese government's prime objective in establishing the NaCSSF was to professionally manage the strategic fund of last resort to supplement the anticipated funding gap in the pension systems when required. An ancillary result lay in building the NaCSSF as the model for the other pension-administration and investment organisations for China.

From the onset, NaCSSF had been able to establish a strong culture of investment professionalism, competency, discipline, and transparency through the ADB and World Bank technical-assistance projects. This had set a significant impact not only on the development of China's pension-plan administration, but also its capital markets more widely. Over the years, some of NaCSSF's investment and risk professionals took up senior positions in the private sector and implemented the same culture and discipline at insurance, fund-management, and other investment organisations.

As at the end of 2015, the NSSF had a total of more than RMB1.9 trillion of assets (approx. US$225 billion) and had achieved an accumulated investment return of RMB790.7 million for the fund since inception, with an average investment yield of 8.82% annually. In addition to the NSSF, the NaCSSF had been given additional responsibility to manage the subsidy from central government to employee's basic pension individual accounts of nine pilot provinces since the end of 2006, as well as part of the surplus of employee's basic pension insurance for some provinces, including Guangdong since 2012 and Shangdong since 2015.[32] This extension of NaCSSF's investment responsibility was one of the key recommendations in our TA projects.

In October 2015, the one-child policy was formally abolished, replaced by a two-child policy.

32 Source: from NaCSSF's official website http://www.ssf.gov.cn/ : 15 July 2016

20. Global Financial Crisis

The Global Financial Crisis in 2008 has often been compared with the Great Depression in the U.S. in the 1930's. But most of us working in the financial industry had only read in books about the Great Depression that happened almost a century ago. The live experience of the 2008 Global Financial Crisis, however, remains very much fresh and vivid in our minds.

On 18 August 2008, I moved from Singapore back to Hong Kong with my family to spearhead the business expansion plan of Northern Trust in North Asia from Hong Kong. The date was most auspicious according to Chinese *fung-shui*, with the number 8 in the day, month and year. But at the end, it did not help to allay what turned out to be a global financial crisis just a month after we settled in.

It was at 7:00 am on Sunday in Hong Kong on 14 September that I received a call from Chicago notifying me to join an urgent conference-call for the global leadership team at 9:00 am to discuss an important market event that would have a grave impact to the market. The senior management of the bank were on their way back to the Chicago head-office. It was a short phone call and did not disclose what exactly the event was, but the gravity of the matter was evident. I went out jogging after hanging up the phone, and did my usual 5-K weekend run to freshen up my mind.

During the conference call, we were briefed that Lehman Brothers, the fourth largest investment bank in the U.S., was on the brink of collapse due to calamitous losses with its huge portfolio of subprime mortgages. Its share price had plummeted from a peak of US$82 in 2007 to less than US$4 following a 42% plunge on 14 September. Lehman was left with only US$1 billion in cash over the weekend. Time was running out.

The US authorities were making last-ditch efforts to facilitate a takeover of the firm by either Barclays PLC. or Bank of America Corp. It was not certain whether the efforts would be successful.

The crisis was triggered by the collapse of the housing bubble in the U.S. after a decade of expansion of the household debt market, financed by mortgage-backed securities (MBS) and collateralised debt obligations (CDO) that peaked in 2004. Cracks in the US housing market started to appear since March 2007 when several mortgage-financing firms in the U.S. filed for Chapter 11 bankruptcy protection in 2007.

Year 2008 started off with more dark clouds in the financial horizon. In February, a domestic mortgage lender in the U.K., Northern Rock, was taken over by the government after having a liquidity crisis for several months.

Then in March, Bear Stearns, one of the top-tier US independent investment banks, was felled by a massive run on its liquidity, as clients and trading partners fled over just a few days fearing that it would not be able to meet its obligations due to its massive losses in asset-backed securities. It was pushed into the arms of JP Morgan by the US authorities on 16 March for a takeover at US$10 per share after a chaotic weekend.

Bear Stearns office in Madison Avenue, New York City; Source: Wikipedia

A credit crunch was forming in the market as a result. The US Fed had to cut interest rates from 5.25% on 28 June 2007, and quickly to 2% on 28 April 2008 with several reductions. A Term Auction Facility (TAF) was created in December 2007 through which fixed amounts of term funds were auctioned to depository institutions against a wide variety of collateral. Another Term Securities Lending Facility (TSLF) was created in March 2008, which would lend Treasury securities against a variety of federal agency debts, residential MBS, and other securities.

But these measures were far from adequate to stop financial institutions loaded with subprime debts to survive.

Lehman would be the second major investment bank globally after Bear Stearns, facing bankruptcy within the year. It was anticipated there would be more bankruptcy to come. The next concern would be Merrill Lynch, the world's largest and most widely recognised stockbroker. With Lehman's demise, attention of investors and speculators would be focusing on Merrill's financial troubles.

Lehman Brothers office in Time Square, New York City; Source: Wikipedia

Most banks and pension funds had dealings with Lehman. Hedge funds also traded extensively with Lehman. The market would be in serious tumult when it opened on Monday. We discussed the contingency plans that had been prepared to manage the potential impact on our business operations as well as plans for communicating to clients.

On Monday 15 September, Merrill Lynch announced it had struck a deal to be acquired by Bank of America for US$29 a share, a 70% premium on its closing price of US$17.05 on Friday but only half of what the firm was worth earlier in the year and a third of its peak at the beginning of 2007.

However, Lehman did not find its white knight and filed for Chapter 11 for bankruptcy protection, resulting in the stock plunging 93% from its previous close on Friday. A takeover bid by Barclays failed to work out because the US authorities refused to provide a guarantee for Lehman's trading obligations as part of a deal to buy the business.

The dramatic collapse of Lehman Brothers shocked the financial markets, with share prices slumping around the world. Unwinding Lehman's complex deals would take months if not years. In the meantime, the global financial system would be snarled up. Banks would not know for sure how much they were exposed to Lehman and would have difficulty freeing up the money in those deals. This in turn intensified the credit crunch, with dire consequences for businesses and consumers.

However, the market was braced for yet another even bigger shock during the week. The insurance giant, American International Group (AIG), was running out of cash to cover its losses and asked the US government for emergency assistance. On 16 September 2008, the federal government gave AIG a bail-out of US$85 billion. In exchange, the US government received 79.9% of the firm's equity. For decades,

AIG had been the world's biggest insurer, a company known around the world for providing protection for individuals, companies and others, but AIG itself would have gone under during the week if it were not for government assistance.

AIG was considered too big to fail. An incredible number of institutional investors - mutual funds, pension funds and hedge funds - both invested in and also were insured by the company. In particular, many investment banks that had CDOs insured by AIG were at risk of losing billions of Dollars. If AIG were to become insolvent, it would send shockwaves through the already shaky money markets because millions of investors - both individuals and institutions - would lose their wealth in what were perceived to be incredibly safe holdings.

AIG Headquarter Building in New York City; Source: Wikipedia

The bail-out was controversial. Some criticised whether or not it was appropriate for the US government to use taxpayer money to purchase a struggling insurance company. In addition, the use of public funds to pay out bonuses to AIG's officials caused uproar. However, others said that the bail-out, if successful, would actually benefit taxpayers due to returns on the government's share of the company's equity.

In the following weeks, many more major financial institutions, not only in the U.S. but also in Europe, reported serious financial troubles and required emergency rescue:

- Halifax Bank of Scotland merged with Lloyds TSB in the U.K. on 17 September.
- Washington Mutual was acquired by JP Morgan Chase on 25 September.
- National City Corp was acquired by PNC Financial Services Group on 24 September.
- German bank Hypo Real Estate required to be bailed out by banks and government on 29 September.
- Fortis Bank was bailed out by the governments of Netherlands, Belgium and Luxembourg on 29 September.
- Iceland bank Glitnir was part-nationalised on 29 September.
- Dexia was bailed out by the governments of France, Belgium and Luxembourg on 30 September.
- Fortis' insurance activities were nationalised by the Dutch government on 3 October.

- 75% stake of Fortis Bank was acquired by BNP Paribas on 6 October.
- Icelandic bank Landsbanki was nationalised on 7 October.
- Icelandic bank Kaupthing was nationalised on 9 October.
- Wachovia was acquired by Wells Fargo on 12 October.
- Royal Bank of Scotland, Lloyds TSB and Halifax Bank of Scotland were bailed out by the UK government on 13 October.
- UBS was bailed out by Swiss government on 16 October.
- Commerce Bancorp was acquired by Canadian bank Toronto-Dominion on 24 October.
- Banco Portuguese de Negocious was nationalised by Portugal government on 2 November.
- Parex Bank was nationalised by Latvia government on 8 November.
- Citigroup was bailed out by US authorities on 28 November.

The crisis had become global. Confidence in financial institutions sank to an all-time low as billions of Dollars of their market capitalisation evaporated with plunges in their stock prices. Custodians were no exceptions. We had to respond to numerous questions about legal, regulatory, and operational questions about asset safety and protection of client assets that were under custody with us should we go down. Many of these questions had no definite answers because there were simply very few previous cases to rely on.

Market tension was extremely high; investor confidence was extremely fragile. Some clients reacted by moving their assets around from one institution to another. Fund managers moved their holdings from one asset class to another and one country to another.

Banks in the Asia Pacific had been faring quite well during the crisis so far, thanks to the efforts to strengthen their capital and liquidity ratios after the Asia financial crisis in 1997-8. No bank required emergency financial rescue despite the plummeting of their stock prices and business revenue. Nonetheless, dozens of banks in Hong Kong and Singapore were soon caught in the Lehman mini-bond scandal after the collapse of investment bank.

Tens of thousands of retail investors in Hong Kong who had spent some HK$20 billion on mini-bonds issued by Lehman saw the value of their investments fell to zero. Similarly, about 10,000 retail investors in Singapore lost all or a large part of their investments totaling over S$500 million in products linked to Lehman. The banks and brokerage firms that distributed the products were accused of having mis-sold these relatively high-risk structured products to the investors, many of whom were housewives and the elderly who thought they had bought into safe deposit-like investments when in fact they had not. Much of the following months was taken up with bitter accusations of mis-selling and inadequate regulation, and sparked rounds of investor activism in both cities. Ultimately, the government authorities in both cities had to intervene under public pressure, and investors managed to receive compensation for part of their investments. It also prompted the regulators to review and tighten sales practices of complex products to non-professional investors, to improve disclosure and client risk-profiling rules.

Liquidity continued to be a big issue with the lack of confidence in financial institutions and the financial system as a whole, despite various capital injections into the market. Governments had to take bolder steps to forestall investor confidence.

On 30 September, the Irish government announced a guarantee of deposits with its banks to preserve stability of its banking system. This was immediately followed by a number of European governments including U.K., Germany, France, Italy, Netherlands, and others. In the Asia Pacific, Australia, New Zealand, Hong Kong, Singapore and Malaysia governments all joined their European counterparts in announcing bank-deposit guarantees soon afterwards.

Each of these deposit-guarantee programmes, however, were different when one deep-dived into the details - the level of guarantee, how it is being guaranteed, to whom the guarantee would apply, etc. But details were often lacking when the announcements were made. Numerous questions were received from clients and we were left with backlogs of many open issues to follow up on.

Most of these market events did not directly hit custodian banks, but eventually one problem arising as a result of the subprime and liquidity crisis did - securities lending.

Historically, securities lending started off as a means for failed trade covering. Over time, it had evolved as a means for custodian banks to help clients enhance returns by putting idle assets to work to produce additional income by lending securities out as the clients' agent to market players who borrowed the securities to implement their investment strategies. The securities were typically lent out by taking cash as collateral, marked to market on daily basis. Custodian banks would then pool the cash and put it into overnight deposits, money market instruments and repos to earn additional income. The total return from the loan fees and the cash reinvestment will then be split between the client and the custodian bank. These securities-lending programmes seemed to be a relatively safe means to produce additional revenue and became very popular among ETFs, mutual funds, pension funds, endowments, and government funds.

Over time, securities lending had become an important and significant business globally. The volume of securities loans grew rapidly. The global volume of securities loans grew from just less than US$600 billion in the mid-1990's to US$2.3 trillion in Q3 of 2008, according to estimates from UK-based consulting firm Data Explorers. The annual lending revenue reported by US mutual funds reached over US$1,000 million in 2007 and by pension funds almost US$500 million[33].

Competition heated up among these agency lending programmes by reducing the portion of the revenue split taken by the custodian. From a typical split of 50/50 or 60/40 in the mid-90's, the revenue split was gradually slashed to 80/20 or 90/10 in 2007-8 in favour of clients. Some custodians even cut deals with their clients to provide custody for free in exchange for revenue earned from clients with large asset pools participating in their securities lending programmes.

However, money had to come from somewhere to cover the costs. In order to produce higher returns, the guidelines of the cash-reinvestment pools of many securities-lending programmes were revised to take additional risk with client's approval, either in the form of longer average-duration risk of the reinvestment pool and/or expanded investment scope to include higher-yield instruments including MBS.

When the subprime debt bubble burst, most of these cash-reinvestment pools dropped below their par values due to the toxic assets in their holdings. Many clients, especially pension funds, did

33 *Securities Lending Market Trends*, September 2009, *Sunguard ASTEC Analytics.*

not expect this to happen and wanted to cut loss by terminating their participation in the programmes immediately, but they were not allowed to do so. The MBS securities had totally lost market liquidity and there were no market prices for them. It was not possible to put a value to these MBS securities. Even if clients were willing to totally write off the value of their share of the MBS holdings in the pool, in order to accommodate them leaving the programme, the good and liquid securities in the pool had to be sold in order to recall the securities on loan. This would negatively impact the liquidity of the programme and its ability to operate, and would be unfair to those clients remaining in the programme. Furthermore, a number of countries had banned short selling during this crisis period and lending activities were much lower than they used to be. It was not easy for the securities-lending programmes to maintain their continuity if there were massive departure by clients.

As a result, custodian banks put gates on their programmes and would not allow participants who had invested their cash collateral in pool funds to leave. Obviously, clients caught in this situation were extremely unhappy. They disputed against the gating measures fiercely. We had to deal with angry customers with their daily complaints. Some claimed that they had been misled in agreeing to investment guidelines that included investing in MBS and they threatened legal action. We had to explain and show evidence that the guidelines had indeed been discussed with them before they signed off those guidelines. Client relationships had never been tenser.

Some clients did sue for compensation in any case: JP Morgan, State Street, Bank of New York, Citibank, and Northern Trust were all involved in lawsuits with clients.[34]

---

34 *State Street Sec-Lending Revenue Drops, Lawsuits Percolate*, 11 March 2011, *Ignites*.

The ferocity of the crisis was like a tsunami gulping up the financial markets and players across the globe. It forced governments around the world to take concerted efforts to implement new initiatives to instill confidence in the financial system while injecting billions of Dollars into the financial systems continuously:

On 8 October, the central banks of the U.S., U.K., China, Canada, Sweden, Switzerland and ECB cut interest rates in a coordinated attempt to ease pressure on borrowers to give a strong signal to the markets of their collective resolve to manage the credit crunch.

On 14 October, Paul Hanson announced the Troubled Asset Relief Plan (TARP) programme to purchase capital from US banks.

On 21 October, the Fed announced the creation of the Money Market Investor Funding Facility (MMIFF) to provide senior secured funding to a series of special-purpose vehicles to facilitate the purchase of assets from eligible investors, such as US money-market mutual funds.

On November 25, the Fed announced the creation of the Term Asset-Backed Securities Lending Facility (TALF) to lend up to US$200 billion on a non-recourse basis to holders of AAA-rated asset-backed securities and recently originated consumer and small-business loans.

These measures to increase money supply in the banking systems were reinforced in stronger doses in the following months in what was known as the 'Quantitative Easing' monetary policy. Eventually, these measures did produce positive impact on the markets despite disagreement on the potential side-effects of such measures. The markets regained liquidity. On 18 September, the US Treasury announced the expiration of the Guarantee Program for Money Market funds and had earned approximately US$1.2 billion in participation fees. On 14 October, the Dow Jones Industrial closed above 10,000 for the first time in twelve months.

The financial industry slowly recovered from the global crisis. Gates on money-market funds, hedge funds, and securities-lending programmes were lifted. Investment and trading activities went back to normal.

There are many lessons to learn. The financial crisis has taught us that the confidence of the financial market, once shattered, cannot be quickly restored. In an interconnected world, a seeming liquidity crisis can very quickly turn into a solvency crisis for financial institutions, a balance of payment crisis for sovereign countries, and a full-blown crisis of confidence for the entire world.

Lehman's collapse (and the subsequent Madoff affair) has proved a reminder once again of the importance of the custodial function in asset protection despite the complex unwinding process involved in the collapse of financial institutions.

The financial crisis has also highlighted custodian banks' role in funding and settling securities transactions in addition to the multiple fiduciary roles they perform on behalf of investors, making them systemically important for the continuous operation of global financial markets. If, for example, one of the top largest global custodians were to become unstable, the effects would create serious disruption to the interbank funding, foreign-exchange, mutual-fund pricing, subscription and redemption processes, and the securities-lending and financing markets. It is therefore no coincidence that the top six custodians in the world were among the first batch of twenty-nine G-SIFI's (Global Systemically Important Financial Institutions) named by the G20 in 2011.

Custodian banks are also the principal source of intraday and short-term credit that enables broker-dealers to settle transactions. If such credit from custodian banks shrank, settlement failures would soar exponentially. Counter-party default procedures would be ignited at multiple CCPs, leading to sales of collateral that might spark a spiral in prices and a flight to quality. Trillions of financial assets, on and off balance sheet, would start to look for a safer haven, taking with them the cash deposits that account for a sizeable proportion of the funding of the balance sheet of the same banks that they are abandoning.

Even though almost all segments of the financial-services industry had been hit hard during the financial crisis, custodian banks had proven to be less affected than investments banks and broker-dealers. For example, layoffs at custodian banks had not been as deep as those at most of the broker-dealers and investment banks.

However, custodian banks are equally facing challenges caused by changes in the global banking environment, especially the endless stream of regulations from across the world that have been introduced as a result of the crisis. With traditional income streams taking a beating in the last couple of years, custodian banks would require transformation to supplement their income by offering innovative services to their clients and achieving operational efficiencies. New opportunities have emerged after the crisis to increase their value-add to clients, for example, by providing services such as collateral optimisation and collateral transformation for capital markets firms, and taking over the securities-processing functions of broker-dealers and investment banks and middle-office functions of investment managers. These services will enable broker-dealers, investment banks or investment managers to keep their costs under control by converting the fixed costs of their non-core functions into variable costs, and focus on activities of strategic importance to achieve time to market in addressing client needs.

The 2008 Global Financial Crisis played a significant role in the failure of key businesses, sharp declines in consumer wealth, prolonged unemployment, and a downturn in economic activities leading to recession across the globe for the next five years, and was a catalyst for the Eurozone sovereign debt crisis.

But there is a silver lining. As in the past, although the process has been painful, markets globally and their participants have come out stronger after the crisis to forge new beginnings. This is certainly true of custodian banks.

Appendix: Timeline of the Global Financial Crisis

2007

February 7, 2007

- HSBC announced losses linked to US subprime mortgages.

May 17, 2007

- Federal Reserve Chairman Ben Bernanke said growing number of mortgage defaults would not seriously harm the US economy.

June, 2007

- Two hedge funds run by Bear Stearns with large holdings of subprime mortgages ran into large losses and were forced to dump assets. The trouble spreads to major Wall Street firms such as Merrill Lynch, JPMorgan Chase, Citigroup and Goldman Sachs which had loaned the firms money.

August 9, 2007

- BNP Paribas froze withdrawals in three investment funds, indicating that they had no way of valuing the complex assets inside them known as collateralised debt obligations (CDOs), or packages of sub-prime loans. It was the first major bank to acknowledge the risk of exposure to sub-prime mortgage markets.

September 2007

- Crisis-hit UK bank Northern Rock admitted financial difficulties as it asked Bank of England for assistance. Share prices fell as customers queued up to withdraw their money.

October 1, 2007

- UBS announced losses linked to US subprime mortgages.

October 5, 2007

- Merrill Lynch reported losses of US$5.5 billion.

October 15, 2007

- Citigroup announced US$6.5 billion third quarter losses.

October 24, 2007

- Merrill Lynch announced losses to be over US$8 billion.

2008

January 2008

- UBS announced fourth quarter losses at US$14 billion.

January 11, 2008

- Bank of America paid US$4 billion for Countryside Financial.

January 15, 2008

- Citigroup reported US$18.1 billion loss in fourth quarter.

January 17, 2008

- Merrill Lynch reported US$11.5 billion loss in fourth quarter. Washington Mutual posted losses.

February 13, 2008

- Northern Rock in the U.K. was nationalised.

March 2008

- UK hedge fund Peloton Partners and US fund Carlyle Capital failed.

March 16, 2008

- Bear Stearns, US's fifth largest investment bank, collapsed and was taken over by JP Morgan.

April 1, 2008

- Deutsche Bank reported losses of US$3.9 billion in first quarter.

April 13, 2008

- Wachovia Corp. reported big loss for quarter.

May 12, 2008

- HSBC wrote off US$3.2 billion in the first quarter linked to exposure to the US subprime market.

July 22, 2008

- Washington Mutual reported US$3.3 billion loss for second quarter.

August 31, 2008

- Commerzbank AG took over Dresdner Kleinwort investment bank.

September 7, 2008

- Fannie Mae and Freddie Mac were effectively nationalised by the US Treasury which placed them into conservatorship.

September 9, 2008

- Lehman Brothers shares plummeted to lowest level on Wall Street in more than a decade.

September 15, 2008

- Lehman Brothers filed for Chapter 11 bankruptcy protection.

- Stock markets plummeted.

- Central banks injected billions of Dollars into money markets.

- Bank of America agreed to buy Merrill Lynch for US$50 billion.

September 16, 2008

- Federal Reserve Bank of New York bailed out American International Group (AIG).

- The net asset value of shares in the Reserve Primary Money Fund fell below US$1.

- Morgan Stanley and Wachovia entered merger talks.

September 17, 2008

- Halifax Bank of Scotland (HBOS) to merge with UK bank Lloyds TSB in an emergency rescue plan.

- The Securities and Exchange Commission (SEC) announced a temporary emergency ban on short selling in the stocks of all companies in the financial sector.

September 18, 2008

- Federal Bank and other central banks injected billions into global markets to help ease the crunch.

September 19, 2008

- The US Treasury Department announced a temporary program that would make available up to US$50 billion from the Exchange Stabilization Fund to guarantee investments in participating money market mutual funds.

September 20, 2008

- The US Treasury Department submitted draft legislation to Congress for authority to purchase troubled assets.

September 21, 2008

- The Federal Reserve Board approved applications of investment banking companies Goldman Sachs and Morgan Stanley to become bank holding companies.

September 22, 2008

- Nomura Holdings bought Lehman's Asian operations for up to US$525 million.

September 25, 2008

- JPMorgan Chase acquired the banking operations of Washington Mutual in a transaction facilitated by the Federal Deposit Insurance Corporation (FDIC).

September 27, 2008

- HSBC announced 1,100 job cuts worldwide.

September 29, 2008

- US Congress rejected a US$700 billion-plan to bail out the US financial system.

- UK's Bradford & Bingley nationalised. Santander to buy deposits for US$38.2 billion.

- German bank Hypo Real Estate to be bailed out by banks and government.

- Citigroup, the world's largest bank, said it would buy Wachovia.

- Belgian giant Fortis was bailed out by Netherlands, Belgium and Luxembourg.

- Royal Bank of Scotland shares lost a fifth of their value.

- Iceland part-nationalised Glitnir, one of its biggest banks.

- US Treasury Department opened its Temporary Guarantee Program for Money Market Funds to provide coverage to shareholders.

- The FDIC announced that Citigroup would purchase the banking operations of Wachovia Corporation with a loss-sharing arrangement between FDIC and Citigroup.

30 September 2008

- The Irish government guaranteed the deposits in its main banks for two years.

- Dexia became the first European bank to be bailed out with a package of €6.4 billion by the Belgian, French and Luxembourg governments.

October 1, 2008

- US Senate passed an amended US$700 billion-bail-out plan.

October 3, 2008

- US Congress passed US$700 billion bail-out; President Bush signed it into law.

- UBS to cut 2000 jobs.

- Dutch government nationalised the banking and insurance activities of Fortis.

- Wells Fargo announced a competing proposal to purchase Wachovia Corporation that would not require assistance from the FDIC.

- US Congress passed, and President Bush signed into law, the Emergency Economic Stabilization Act of 2008, which established the US$700 billion Troubled Asset Relief Program (TARP).

October 4-6, 2008

- Proposed Hypo Real Estate bail-out collapsed.

- Chancellor Angela Merkel announced new plan for Hypo bail-out worth US$69 billion.

- Merkel also announced guarantee of deposits in German banks

- UK raised limit on guaranteed bank deposits from £35,000 to £50,000.

- EU leaders met in Paris for emergency summit to discuss financial crisis.

- Battle raged between Citigroup and Wells Fargo over purchase of Wachovia.

- BNP Paribas took 75% stake in Fortis.

October 6, 2008

- Danish government announced plan to guarantee bank deposits.

- Wells Fargo and Citigroup agreed to legal standstill in battle for Wachovia.

- Bank of America reported 68% profit drop, stock sale to raise US$10 billion.

October 7, 2008

- The Federal Reserve Board announced the creation of the Commercial Paper Funding Facility (CPFF) to provide a liquidity backstop to US issuers of commercial paper through a special-purpose vehicle that would purchase three-month unsecured and asset-backed commercial paper directly from eligible issuers.

- The FDIC announced an increase in deposit insurance coverage to US$250,000 per depositor as authorised by the Emergency Economic Stabilization Act of 2008.

- Icelandic bank Landsbanki nationalised; Icesave, Landbanki's internet bank, froze UK customers' accounts.

October 8, 2008

- The Federal Reserve Board authorised the Federal Reserve Bank of New York to borrow up to US$37.8 billion in investment-grade, fixed-income securities from American International Group (AIG) in return for cash collateral. The Federal Reserve Board votes to reduce the primary credit rate 50 basis points to 1.75

- UK Treasury froze assets of Landsbanki in the U.K., threatened legal action.

- UK Treasury announced £500 billion bank rescue package.

- U.S., U.K., China, Canada, Sweden, Switzerland and ECB cut interest rates in a coordinated attempt to ease pressure on borrowers.

- IMF forecasted Major global downturn.

October 9, 2008

- Iceland nationalised its biggest bank Kaupthing.

- October 10, 2008 (Black Friday)

- G7 finance ministers met in Washington and issue a five-point plan.

- Nikkei fell almost 10%, biggest drop in twenty years.

- FTSE fell more than 10%, closed at 8.85%; worst daily fall since 1987.

- Oil prices fell to US$80 a barrel.

- Dow crashed nearly 700 points before regaining some lost ground.

October 11-12, 2008

- The Fed rubber-stamped Wachovia takeover by Wells Fargo.

- Fifteen EU leaders met in Paris for emergency summit on crisis.

- Gordon Brown urged them to adopt similar measures to UK bank rescue plan. Leaders agreed to guarantee loans between banks until end of 2009.

- Germany, France and Italy to announce individual plans Monday.

- Australia agreed to guarantee deposits for next three years.

- New Zealand guaranteed bank deposits for two years.

October 13, 2008

- EU stock markets bounced back in response to EU leaders' bail-out announcements.

- UK bailed out three banks: RBS, HBOS and Lloyds TSB at the cost of US$63 billion.

- Bank of England loaned US$174 million to Icelandic bank Landsbanki to help repay UK depositors.

October 14, 2008

- Paul Hanson pushed through the Troubled Asset Relief Program (TARP) to purchase capital in financial institutions.

- The FDIC created a new Temporary Liquidity Guarantee Program to guarantee the senior debt of all FDIC-insured institutions and their holding companies, as well as deposits in non-interest-bearing deposit transaction.

- Iceland in talks with Russia to negotiate emergency loan of US$5.44 billion after bank collapses.

October 15, 2008

- European and Asian stock markets fell after initial upswing.

- Southeast Asian nations agreed to start fund to provide financial support to countries in crisis; World Bank committed US$10 billion to the planned fund.

- Russian stock market posted losses as RTS Index falls below 800 points.

October 16, 2008

- Global markets fell on fears of global slowdown.
- Citigroup delayed merger of its Japanese brokerage units due to costs involved.
- Swiss government bailed out UBS with US$59.2 billion.
- Credit Suisse posted 1.3 billion-franc third quarter loss; raised US$8.7 billion from investors.
- Hungarian central bank got cash injection from ECB to value of US$6.7 billion.
- EU leaders at Brussels summit called for complete overhaul of international financial system.

October 21, 2008

- The Federal Reserve Board announced creation of the Money Market Investor Funding Facility (MMIFF) to provide senior secured funding to a series of special-purpose vehicles to facilitate the purchase of assets from eligible investors, such as US money market mutual funds.

October 22, 2008

- Barnsley Building Society in the U.K. acquired by Yorkshire Building Society.

October 24, 2008

- PNC Financial Services Group Inc. purchased National City Corporation, creating the fifth largest US bank.
- Commerce Bancorp acquired by Toronto-Dominion Bank.

- UK economy shrank for the first time in sixteen years between July and September as economic growth fell by 0.5%.

October 29, 2008

- The IMF announced the creation of a short-term liquidity facility for market-access countries.

November 2, 2008

- Banco Portuguese de Negocios in Portugal nationalised.

November 4, 2008

- Scarborough Building Society in the U.K. acquired by Skipton Building Society.

November 6, 2008

- IMF approved a US$16.4 billion loan to Ukraine to bolster its economy, which had been shaken by global financial turmoil.

November 7, 2008

- Figures showed that 240,000 Americans lost their jobs in October.

November 8, 2008

- Parex Bank nationalised by Latvia government.

November 9, 2008

- China set out a two-year US$586 billion economic stimulus package to help boost the economy by investing in infrastructure and social projects and by cutting corporate taxes.

November 10, 2008

- The Federal Reserve Board approved the applications of American Express and American Express Travel Related Services to become bank holding companies.

November 14, 2008

- The Eurozone officially slipped into recession after EU figures show that the economy shrank by 0.2% in the third quarter.

- The G20 met for the first time since Lehman's went under, in a meeting that was compared in significance to the Bretton Woods summit in 1944.

November 17, 2008

- Three large US life-insurance companies, Lincoln National, Hartford Financial Services Group, and Genworth Financial, announced their intention to purchase lenders/depositories and thus qualify as savings and loan companies to access TARP funding.

November 20, 2008

- The IMF approves a US$2.1 billion loan for Iceland.

November 21, 2008

- The US Treasury Department announced to help liquidate the Reserve Fund's US Government Fund by serving as a buyer of last resort for the fund's securities to ensure the orderly liquidation of the fund.

November 23, 2008

- The US Treasury Department, Federal Reserve Board, and FDIC jointly announced a bail-out agreement with Citigroup to provide a package of guarantees, liquidity access and capital.

November 25, 2008

- The Federal Reserve Board announced the creation of the Term Asset-Backed Securities Lending Facility (TALF) to lend up to US$200 billion on a non-recourse basis to holders of AAA-rated asset-backed securities and recently originated consumer and small-business loans.

- The US. Treasury would provide US$20 billion of TARP money for credit protection.

November 26, 2008

- The European Commission unveiled an economic recovery plan worth €200 billion.

- The Federal Reserve Board announced approval of Bank of America Corporation's acquisition of Merrill Lynch and Company.

December 1, 2008

- US officially declared entering into recession with figures from National Bureau of Economic Research.

December 3, 2008

- The SEC approved measures to increase transparency and accountability at credit rating agencies and thereby ensure that firms provide more meaningful ratings and greater disclosure to investors.

December 4, 2008

- France announced a €26 billion stimulus plan.

December 15, 2008

- The Federal Reserve Board announced approval of the application of PNC Financial Services to acquire National City Corporation.

December 19, 2008

- The US Treasury Department authorised loans of up to US$13.4 billion for General Motors and US$4.0 billion for Chrysler from the TARP.

December 22, 2008

- The Federal Reserve Board approved the application of CIT Group Inc., a US$81 billion financing company, to become a bank holding company.

December 24, 2008

- The Federal Reserve Board approved the applications of GMAC LLC and IB Finance Holding Company, LLC (IBFHC) to become bank holding companies.

December 29, 2008

- The US Treasury Department announced to purchase US$5 billion in equity from GMAC as part of its program to assist the domestic automotive industry.

December 30, 2008

- The Federal Reserve Board announced they would begin to purchase mortgage-backed securities backed by Fannie Mae, Freddie Mac and Ginnie Mae under a previously announced program in early January 2009.

December 30, 2008

- The US Securities and Exchange Commission (SEC) released a report recommending against the suspension of fair value accounting standards. The report was mandated by the Emergency Economic Stabilization Act of 2008 (EESA).

2009

January 5, 2009

- The Federal Reserve Bank of New York began purchasing fixed-rate mortgage-backed securities guaranteed by Fannie Mae, Freddie Mac and Ginnie Mae.

January 8, 2009

- Moody's Investor Services issued a report suggesting that the Federal Home Loan Banks were facing the potential for significant accounting write-downs on their US$76.2 billion private-label MBS securities portfolio. According to Moody's, only four of 12 Banks' capital ratios would remain above regulatory minimums under a worst-case scenario.

January 9, 2009

- Official figures showed US jobless rate rose to 7.2% in December, the highest in 16 years.

January 13, 2009

- China's exports registered the biggest decline in a decade.

January 15, 2009

- Anglo Irish Bank nationalised by Irish government.

January 16, 2009

- The US Treasury Department, Federal Reserve, and FDIC announced a bail-out package of guarantees, liquidity access, and capital for Bank of America.

- The US Treasury Department, Federal Reserve and FDIC finalised terms of their guarantee agreement with Citigroup.

- The US Treasury Department announced that it would lend US$1.5 billion from the TARP to a special-purpose entity created by Chrysler Financial to finance the extension of new consumer auto loans.

January 23, 2009

- U.K. entered into recession as fourth quarter GDP falls by 1.5% compared to the previous three months.

January 28, 2009

- The National Credit Union Administration (NCUA) Board announced that the NCUA would guarantee uninsured shares at all corporate credit unions through February 2009 and establish a voluntary guarantee program for uninsured shares of credit unions through December 2010.

February 3, 2009

- BTA Bank and Alliance Bank nationalised by Kazakhstan government.

February 6, 2009

- The Federal Reserve Board released additional terms and conditions of the Term Asset-Backed Securities Loan Facility (TALF) to lend up to US$200 billion to eligible owners of certain AAA-rated asset-backed securities backed by newly and recently originated auto loans, credit card loans, student loans and SBA-guaranteed small-business loans.

February 10, 2009

- The US Treasury announced a Financial Stability Plan involving Treasury purchases of convertible preferred stock in eligible banks, the creation of a Public-Private Investment Fund to acquire troubled loans and other assets from financial institutions, expansion of the Federal Reserve's TALF, and new initiatives to stem residential mortgage foreclosures and to support small-business lending.

- The Federal Reserve Board announced that it was prepared to expand the TALF to as much as US$1 trillion and broaden the eligible collateral to include AAA-rated commercial mortgage-backed securities, private-label residential mortgage-backed securities, and other asset-backed securities. An expansion of the TALF would be supported by US$100 billion from the TARP.

February 11, 2009

- Ireland government injected 7 billion into Bank of Ireland and Allied Irish.

February 17, 2009

- President Obama signed into law the American Recovery and Reinvestment Act of 2009, which includes a variety of spending measures and tax cuts intended to promote economic recovery.

February 18, 2009

- President Obama announced The Homeowner Affordability and Stability Plan, including a program to permit the refinancing of conforming home mortgages owned or guaranteed by Fannie Mae or Freddie Mac that currently exceed 80% of the value of the underlying home.

- The U.S. Treasury Department would increase its preferred stock purchase agreements with Fannie Mae and Freddie Mac to US$200 billion, and increase the limits on the size of Fannie Mae and Freddie Mac's portfolios to US$900 billion.

February 21, 2009

- Bank of Antigua bailed out by Eastern Caribbean Central Bank.

February 23, 2009

- US authorities issued a joint statement that the US government stood firmly behind the banking system, and that the government would ensure that banks had the capital and liquidity they needed to provide the credit necessary to restore economic growth. Further, the agencies reiterated their determination to preserve the stability of systemically important financial institutions.

February 25, 2009

- The Federal Reserve Board, Federal Deposit Insurance Corporation, Office of the Comptroller of the Currency and Office of Thrift Supervision announced that they would conduct forward-looking economic assessments or stress tests of eligible US bank holding companies with assets exceeding US$100 billion. Supervisors would work with the firms to estimate the range of possible future losses and the resources to absorb such losses over a two-year period. The assessment process was expected to be completed by the end of April 2009.

February 26, 2009

- The FDIC announced that the number of problem banks increased to 252 insured institutions with US$159 billion in assets at the end of fourth quarter of 2008.

- The FDIC also announced that there were 25 bank failures and five assistance transactions in 2008, which was the largest annual number since 1993.

February 26, 2009

- Fannie Mae reported a loss of US$25.2 billion in the fourth quarter of 2008, and a full-year 2008 loss of US$58.7 billion.

March 2, 2009

- HSBC Finance Corporation announced shutdown of US consumer banking.

March 3, 2009

- The US Treasury Department and the Federal Reserve Board announced the launch of the Term Asset-Backed Securities Loan Facility (TALF).

March 9, 2009

- Islandic bank Straumur Investment Bank bailed out by Iceland government.

March 11, 2009

- Freddie Mac announced that it had a net loss of US$23.9 billion in the fourth quarter of 2008, and a net loss of US$50.1 billion for 2008 as a whole.

March 17, 2009

- The Federal Deposit Insurance Corporation (FDIC) decided to extend the debt guarantee portion of the Temporary Liquidity Guarantee Program (TLGP) from June 30, 2009 through October 31, 2009, and to impose a surcharge on debt issued with a maturity of one-year or more beginning in the second quarter of 2009 to gradually phase-out the program.

March 18, 2009

- The FOMC voted to maintain the target range for the effective federal funds at 0 to 0.25 percent.

- In addition, the FOMC decided to increase the size of the Federal Reserve's balance sheet by purchasing up to an additional US$750 billion of agency mortgage-backed securities, bringing its total purchases of these securities to up to US$1.25 trillion this year, and to increase its purchases of agency debt this year by up to US$100 billion to a total of up to US$200 billion.

- The FOMC also decided to purchase up to US$300 billion of longer-term Treasury securities over the next six months to help improve conditions in private credit markets.

March 19, 2009

- The US Department of the Treasury announced an Auto Supplier Support Program that will provide up to US$5 billion in financing to the automotive industry.

- The Federal Reserve Board announced an expansion of the eligible collateral for loans extended by the Term Asset-Backed Securities Loan Facility (TALF) to include asset-backed securities backed by mortgage servicing advances, loans or leases related to business equipment, leases of vehicle fleets, and floorplan loans.

- The amount of TALF loans requested at the March 17-19 operation was US$4.7 billion.

- The FDIC completed the sale of IndyMac Federal Bank to OneWest Bank.

March 23, 2009

- The Federal Reserve and the US Treasury issue a joint statement on the appropriate roles of each during the current financial crisis and into the future, and on the steps necessary to ensure financial and monetary stability.

- The US Treasury Department announced details for the creation of individual Public-Private Investment Funds to purchase distressed loans that were held by banks.

- The US Treasury Department would approve up to five asset managers to raise private capital to acquire distressed securities currently held by banks.

March 26, 2009

- The US Treasury Department outlined a framework for assigning responsibility over all systemically important firms and critical payment and settlement systems to a single independent regulator.

- It called for higher standards on capital and risk management for systemically important firms; for requiring all hedge funds above a certain size to register with a financial regulator; for a comprehensive framework of oversight, protection and disclosure for the over-the-counter derivatives market; for new requirements for money market funds; and for stronger resolution authority covering all financial institutions that pose systemic risks to the economy.

March 31, 2009

- The US Treasury Department announces an extension of its temporary Money Market Funds Guarantee Program through September 18, 2009.

- Four bank holding companies announced that they had redeemed all of the preferred shares that they had issued to the US Treasury under the Capital Purchase Program of the TARP.

April 2, 2009

- The G20 agreed on a global stimulus package worth US$5 trillion.

May 1, 2009

- One of the big three US carmakers, Chrysler, filed for bankruptcy protection.

May 7, 2009

- The Federal Reserve released the results of a stress test of the nineteen largest US bank holding companies. The assessment found that the nineteen firms could lose US$600 billion during 2009 and 2010 if the economy were to track the more adverse scenario considered in the program. Ten firms would need to add US$185 billion to their capital to maintain adequate buffers under the more adverse scenario.

May 8, 2009

- Fannie Mae reported a loss of US$23.2 billion for the first quarter of 2009.

May 12, 2009

- Freddie Mac reported a first quarter 2009 loss of US$9.9 billion, and a net worth deficit of US$6.0 billion as of March 31, 2009.

May 13, 2009

- The US Treasury Department proposed that all standardised OTC derivatives be cleared through regulated central counterparties, and that all OTC derivatives dealers and all other firms whose activities in those markets creating large exposures to counterparties be subject to prudential supervision and regulation.

May 20, 2009

- President Obama signed the Helping Families Save Their Homes Act of 2009, which temporarily raised FDIC deposit insurance coverage from US$100,000 per depositor to US$250,000 per depositor. The new coverage at FDIC-insured institutions would expire on January 1, 2014.

May 21, 2009

- Standard and Poor's Ratings Services lowered its outlook on the United Kingdom government debt from stable to negative because of the estimated fiscal cost of supporting the nation's banking system.

May 27, 2009

- The FDIC announced that the number of problem banks increased to 305 institutions with US$220 billion of assets at the end of the first quarter of 2009.

- There were twenty-one bank failures in the first quarter of 2009, which was the largest number of failed institutions in a quarter since the first quarter of 1992.

June 1, 2009

- The world's largest carmaker, GM, filed for bankruptcy protection.

June 5, 2009

- The US Treasury purchased a total of US$40 million in preferred stock from three US banks under the Capital Purchase Program.

June 9, 2009

- The US Treasury Department announced that ten of the largest US financial institutions participating in the Capital Purchase Program had met the requirements for repayment established by the primary federal banking supervisors.

- UK unemployment rate rises to 7.1% with 2.22 million people out of work in the first three months of 2009

June 25, 2009

- AIG announced that it had entered into an agreement with the Federal Reserve Bank of New York to reduce the debt AIG owes the Federal Reserve Bank of New York by US$25 billion

July 15, 2009

- Congress announced the appointment of members to the Financial Crisis Inquiry Commission.

July 16, 2009

- China's economy grew at an annual rate of 7.9% between April and June, up from 6.1% in the first quarter, thanks to the government's big stimulus package

July 21, 2009

- Bernanke testified that the extreme risk aversion of last fall has eased somewhat, and investors are returning to private credit markets.

July 24, 2009

- The Federal Reserve announced that the amounts of Term Auction Facility (TAF) credit offered at each of the two auctions in August will be reduced to US$100 billion from US$125 billion in July.

August 6, 2009

- Fannie Mae reported a loss of US$14.8 billion in the second quarter of 2009.

August 27, 2009

- The FDIC announced that the number of problem banks increased to 416 institutions with US$299.8 billion of assets at the end of the second quarter of 2009.

August 28, 2009

- The Federal Reserve announced that the amounts of TAF credit offered at each of the two auctions in September would be reduced to US$75 billion from US$100 billion in August.

September 18, 2009

- The US Department of the Treasury announced the expiration of the Guarantee Program for Money Market Funds, which was implemented in the wake of the failure of Lehman Brothers in September 2008.

- Since its inception, the Treasury had no losses under the Program and earned approximately US$1.2 billion in participation fees.

October 14, 2009

- The Dow Jones Industrial Average closed above 10,000 for the first time since October 3, 2008.

November 5, 2009

- Fannie Mae reported a net loss of US$18.9 billion in the third quarter of 2009.

November 9, 2009

- The Federal Reserve Board announced that nine of the ten bank holding companies that were determined earlier this year to need to raise capital or improve the quality of their capital now had increased their capital sufficiently to meet or exceed their required capital buffers.

November 17, 2009

- Citing continued improvement in financial-market conditions, the Federal Reserve Board approved a reduction in the maximum maturity of primary credit loans at the discount window for depository institutions to twenty-eight days from ninety days, effective January 14, 2010.

December 2, 2009

- Bank of America announced the repurchase of the entire US$45 billion of cumulative preferred stock issued to the US Treasury under the TARP after the completion of a securities offering.

December 9, 2009

- US Treasury Secretary Timothy Geithner outlined the Administration's exit strategy for the TARP.

December 14, 2009

- Citigroup announced that it had reached an agreement with the US Government to repay the remaining US$20 billion in TARP trust preferred securities issued to the US Treasury.

December 14, 2009

- Wells Fargo announced to redeem the US$25 billion of preferred stock issued to the US Treasury under the TARP, upon successful completion of a US$10.4 billion common stock offering.

2010

February 1, 2010

- The Commercial Paper Funding Facility, Asset-Backed Commercial Paper Money Market Mutual Fund Liquidity Facility, Primary Dealer Credit Facility, and Term Securities Lending Facility programs expired.

February 18, 2010

- The Federal Reserve Board announced an increase in the discount rate from ½% to ¾%, effective February 19, 2010.

February 23, 2010

- The FDIC announced that the number of problem banks to 702 institutions with US$402.8 billion of assets at the end of the fourth quarter of 2009.

February 24, 2010

- Freddie Mac reported a net loss of US$6.5 billion in the fourth quarter of 2009 and a full-year 2009 net loss of US$21.6 billion, compared with a US$50.1 billion net loss in 2008.

February 26, 2010

- Fannie Mae reported a net loss of US$15.2 billion in the fourth quarter of 2009 and a full-year 2009 loss of US$72.0 billion.

April 27, 2010

- Greek debt downgraded to junk.

May 5, 2010

- Freddie Mac reported a net loss of US$6.7 billion in the first quarter of 2010, compared with a US$6.5 billion net loss in the fourth quarter of 2009.

May 10, 2010

- Fannie Mae reported a net loss of US$11.5 billion in the first quarter of 2010, compared with a net loss of US$15.2 billion in the fourth quarter of 2009.

June 11, 2010

- The US Department of the Treasury announced that TARP repayments to taxpayers have, for the first time, surpassed the total amount of TARP funds outstanding.

July 21, 2010

- President Barack Obama signed the Dodd-Frank Wall Street Reform and Consumer Protection Act, Public Law 111-203 into law to promote financial stability in the United States through a variety of mechanisms.

October 5, 2010

- The US Department of the Treasury released a two-year retrospective report on TARP providing a comprehensive overview of the steps that Treasury took under TARP to contain a growing financial panic that gripped the country in late 2008 and early 2009.

2011

January 27, 2011

- The Financial Crisis Inquiry Commission released its final report on the causes of the financial and economic crisis in the United States.

February 11, 2011

- The US Treasury Department and the Department of Housing and Urban Development released their report to Congress on Reforming America's Housing Finance Market.

Source:

*Financial Crisis: Full timeline, Federal Reserve Bank of St Louis (*https://www.stlouisfed.org/financial-crisis/full-timeline);

List of banks acquired or bankrupted during the Great Recession, Wikipedia;

Financial Crisis: Timeline, the Guardian (http://www.theguardian.com/business/2012/aug/07/credit-crunch-boom-bust-timeline);

Timeline: Credit crunch to downturn, BBC News (http://news.bbc.co.uk/2/hi/business/7521250.stm)

21. The RMB Speed Train

RMB internationalisation has been a buzz word since the 2008 global financial crisis. The speed train from China to promote the RMB as a global currency has been travelling with dazzling momentum.

The 2008 crisis hit hard at the economy of the U.S. and spilled over to Europe. The Asia region, on the other hand, had weathered the storm relatively unscathed and emerged from the crisis quickly. This has given rise to the idea that the global economic centre of gravity is shifting from the West to the East. It is seen that the Asian region, with China at its forefront, is assuming an ever more important role in the wider world economy, so much so that it is predicted that the twenty-first century will be the beginning of a new Asian Century.

The starting point for serious discussion of RMB internationalisation can be traced back to 23 March 2009 when the People's Bank of China (PBOC) released a speech by its Governor, Zhou Xiao-Chuan, calling for reform of the international reserve system.[35] He drew attention to weaknesses of the current international monetary system, which he argued was too reliant on holding sovereign currency reserves in US Dollars. He urged expanding the use of the IMF's Special Drawing Rights (SDR) and proposed a stronger international role for the RMB in the valuation of SDR.

The global financial crisis in 2008 was made in the U.S. and exported from the U.S. Some critics began to raise serious concerns about the credibility of the US Dollar and its exorbitant privilege. With unconventional monetary policy and Quantitative Easing phase 1, 2, & 3 in progress, there were increasing doubts by some

35 *Reform of the International Monetary System*, 23 March 2009, *People's Bank of China. http://www.pbc.gov.cn/english/130724/2842945/index.html*

commentators whether the U.S. could ever fulfil its total public-debt obligation, which had exceeded its GDP by over 200% and was still growing. Some countries around the world questioned the unfair advantage of the US Dollar in lowering the cost of debt to the U.S., in terms of financing cost, transaction cost, and ability to externalise its debts.

The crisis had revealed weaknesses and vulnerabilities in the existing global financial system, but the crisis had affected China much less than other major economies. It had become evident to Chinese policymakers the importance of its stronger control over key financial variables and capital movements for the continued growth of the country.

Governor Zhou's speech was released shortly after the US central bank's Quantitative Easing program, which was perceived by many developing countries as contributing to more instability in global financial markets and as accentuating pressures on them to appreciate their currencies.

Prior to this, China had made several initiatives for limited relaxation of capital-controls. In November 2002, the Qualified Financial Institutional Investor (QFII) programme was introduced, being China's first effort to allow, on a very selective basis, global institutional investors to invest in its RMB-denominated A-Shares on the Shanghai and Shenzhen stock exchanges. It was one of the most significant milestones for China's financial reforms in opening up its capital market to overseas investors.

'When I was invited by former Premier Zhu Rong-Ji as the chief advisor for the China Securities Regulatory Commission (CSRC) in late 1998, one of my first major jobs was to assist the market to develop a robust institutional investment community,' said Francis Neoh, former chairman of Securities and Futures Commission in Hong Kong in 1995-98, who is acclaimed as the father of the QFII scheme.[36]

'I found the Hong Kong model was ill-fitted to China as it lacked "Hong Kong market cultures" and I eventually decided to employ the Taiwanese model in the 80s because of its affinity to Chinese culture and mechanisms,' commented Mr. Neoh.

Eligible investors would have to first convert foreign currency to RMB before placing the funds with an approved custodian. Profits from the investments would have to be converted back to foreign currency before being repatriated out of the country under strict controls. Qualified investors would need to have at least US$10 billion in AUM as the Chinese regulators wanted to lure only the market leaders to joining the scheme.

UBS and Nomura Securities were the first two institutions that received approved quotas of US$300 million and US$50 million respectively in June 2003, followed by ten other large investment banks in the same year. Although the quota amounts were only several hundred million US Dollars in total, they were goldmines for generating profits. Smaller firms had to rent quota from them at a high premium in order to invest in China's stock markets. Total quota on QFII increased from US$2.175 billion in 2003 to almost US$13 billion in mid-2008.

In 2004, the Qualified Domestic Institutional Investor (QDII) programme was launched for Chinese insurance companies to invest their foreign-exchange funds in the Chinese companies traded in overseas markets. PingAn insurance company was the first institutional investor to receive a QDII quota of US$8.89 billion.

36 *The liberalisation of China's capital market*, 20th Anniversary 2015 Issue, *Asia Asset Management*.

During the same year, RMB deposits were allowed in Hong Kong and have since seen the deposit base gradually grow from RMB12 billion to RMB59 billion in 2009.

In April 2006, the QDII programme was expanded to other Chinese institutions, allowing retail clients to go through Chinese commercial banks to invest in fixed-income and money-market products. All the participants in the programme were required to first obtain a QDII license from the relevant regulatory agency (either the Securities, Banking or Insurance Regulatory Commission) and then a quota, which was granted by the State Administration of Foreign Exchange (SAFE) as the first step of their overseas investment. The first bank to receive a QDII quota was the Bank of China with US$1 billion of quota, and the first fund approved was Huaan Fund Management with a quota of US$500 million. The QDII investment scope was widened in May 2007 to stock related products as long as the net value of a QDII product investing in stocks would not exceed 50%.

However, the QDII programme was ill-timed. Total quota of US$14.2 billion was granted for investing overseas when the programme was first launched in April 2006. It quickly grew to US$64.5 billion as at end of 2007. However, due to the global financial turmoil, the programme was suspended in the second half-year of 2008 and no quota was approved until the programme was restarted in May 2009. Many people who invested in the first batches of QDII funds had been sitting on huge losses in net asset value for years when the market collapsed globally following the Lehman crisis and did not recover until global stock markets were restored to their former peaks in 2014-5.

To attract investors in RMB-denominated products, *dim-sum* bonds were introduced in Hong Kong - bonds issued outside of China but denominated in Chinese Renminbi. They are named after the popular

Hong Kong dumplings, *dim-sum*, which are very tasty but served in small portions - referring to the small size of each bond issue. The first dim-sum bond was issued by the China Development Bank in July 2007.

These initiatives to facilitate the investment inflows and outflows of China created a source of new and welcomed business opportunities to investment managers and custodians, especially those based in Hong Kong. The QFII programme was targeted at foreign investors, who typically hired foreign managers and custodians for a strong understanding of their needs. While the QDII programme was targeted at domestic Chinese investors and the investments were directed to foreign markets, domestic Chinese institutions typically used foreign fund managers as advisors and foreign custodians as global sub-custodian. Those custodians who were well positioned for these initiatives enjoyed very significant first mover advantage.

However, despite these initiatives, much of the cross-border movements of RMB were still exchange-rate arbitration rather than a true market-driven use of the RMB as an international currency. The global financial crisis triggered the opportune time for China to embark on a much more proactive journey on RMB internationalisation. Chinese policy makers have since been piloting a variety of experiments to internationalise the RMB as a trade settlement currency, an investment currency and a reserve currency.

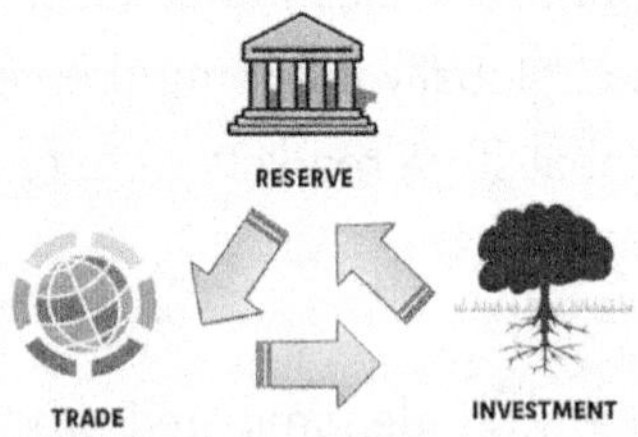

The three components of RMB internationalisation development; Source: BNP Paribas

Since 2009, China have signed currency swap agreements with twenty-four central banks in addition to South Korea with the total amount of over RMB2.7 trillion. It also implemented schemes between Chinese trading cities and foreign countries enabling RMB to be used to settle trade payments. By December 2013, RMB overtook the Euro to become the second-most-used currency in global trade finance after the US Dollar, according to the Society for Worldwide Interbank Financial Telecommunication (SWIFT).

To bolster the RMB's status as an investment currency and a reserve currency, China introduced several ground-breaking initiatives to further open up its capital markets on its journey of RMB internationalisation.

At a forum in Hong Kong on 7 August 2011, the vice-premier at that time, Li Ke-Qiang, announced the RMB Qualified Financial Institutional Investors (RQFII) Scheme, allowing Hong Kong subsidiaries of mainland asset-management firms to be licensed and given quota to raise funds from investors in Hong Kong with RMB offshore deposits for investing into the mainland securities market. The initial quota limit was RMB20 billion. Most of these Hong Kong subsidiaries were newly established. This scheme would give them a head-start in the market to offer a unique product to tap on the RMB620 billion offshore deposits in Hong Kong, to the jealousy of foreign asset managers.

I joined BNP Paribas Group in April 2010 as the Asia Pacific CEO of its subsidiary bank, BNP Paribas Securities Services (BPSS). BNP Paribas is a universal bank that has a long history and diverse business lines in the region, with local presence in 14 countries employing over 7,000 staff.

BPSS was established in late 1995 through the acquisition of the multi-local custody business of Morgan Guaranty Trust by Banque

Paribas (please refer to the Prologue). Banque Paribas merged with Banque Nationale de Paris in 2000, and BPSS became the wholly owned subsidiary of the Group.

The bank was growing very rapidly in Europe. At the end of 2007 (just over twelve years after establishment), it overtook HSBC as the largest custodian in Europe in assets under custody and the fifth largest in the world. In the Asia Pacific, however, while it had a presence in Australia and New Zealand, the business was a new start-up in Asia and a very late comer versus competition by at least fifteen to twenty-five years. The Singapore Branch was set up in late 2008 and Hong Kong Branch obtained its license in 2009. My mission was to build a new business platform off the ground in Asia and to consolidate the existing business in Australia and New Zealand as part of the region.

China is definitely a strategic market for BNP Paribas. Like other custodian banks, we were very keen to participate in this new RQFII initiative. The first batch of funds was targeted to be launched at the end of the year, even though the scheme was only announced in August. The time-line was really very tight. However, the pilot implementation measures, especially the process of converting offshore CNH to onshore CNY for investing under the scheme, were not available until 16 December. This gave Bank of China (BOC) a unique advantage. Asset management firms believed that they would have the direct and easier means of resolving any CNH/CNY currency management issues by using BOC as custodian for the funds, given its role as the RMB clearing and settlement bank for Hong Kong. As a result, all the nine firms approved in the first batch appointed BOC as custodian for the RQFII funds.

The first two RQFII products, managed by the subsidiaries of Haitong Securities and China Universal Asset Management, were finally launched on 11 January 2012 and received overwhelming public subscription. Foreign custodians, like foreign asset managers, were not able to play any role.

It was not until the launch of the second and third batch of funds that foreign custodians got their share of activities. Foreign fund managers were eventually also covered by the scheme in March 2013 to launch RQFII funds domiciled in Hong Kong.

In October 2014, the RQFII scheme was expanded beyond Hong Kong, with U.K. becoming the first country to get a quota, followed by Singapore. Since then, the scheme has expanded to other countries such as Korea, Luxembourg, France, Germany, Switzerland, Saudi Arabia, Australia, Canada and the U.S. Hong Kong remained by far the largest of any offshore RMB market, both in terms of quota and number of RQFII funds, including RQFII ETFs.

In early 2014, another ground-breaking initiative, the Shanghai-Hong Kong Stock Connect, was announced, enabling international investors to access stocks listed on the Shanghai Stock Exchange offshore through the Hong Kong Stock Exchange without the requirement to apply for an individual quota. Similarly, qualified mainland investors would also be able to access certain Hong Kong listed stocks through the Shanghai Stock Exchange.

This was another excellent business opportunity for BNP Paribas. After establishing in the market for several years, we were able to build a strong reputation in clearing and custody services in Hong Kong among clients in APAC and outside the region. At the same time, the securities brokerage arm of the Group in Hong Kong was also very keen to leverage this initiative to tap client interest in the Chinese A-Shares. We decided to join our efforts to launch a seamless integrated execution to clearing and settlement solution after studying the operational process of the scheme. Our solution would address the investors' concern with counterparty risk and information risk associated with the A-Shares market practice in China of delivering shares free of payment to brokers on T+0 and receiving cash on T+1. Our solution would ensure delivery versus payment within our custody system on T+1 for clients executing the trades through the brokerage arm of BNP Paribas and settling those trades with BPSS as custodian.

The scheme was launched on 17 November 2014 after months of anticipation and several market simulation tests. The north-bound gross market trading limit was 100% filled by mid-day on the first day of trading, but trading volumes have not reached the daily gross limit since then due to market sentiments of the A-Share market.

Launch of the Shanghai-Hong Kong Stock Connect on 17 November 2014;

Source: Author's photo collection

For the first year of operation, Shanghai stocks attracted RMB121 billion (US$19.73 billion) through the scheme, about 40% of the aggregate quota, according to the Shanghai Stock Exchange. Hong

Kong stocks attracted RMB92.4 billion through the programme, about 37% of the annual quota, according to the Hong Kong Exchange.

The integrated solution that we launched for the Stock Connect enjoyed good success. BNP Paribas was one of the only three providers in the market that provided an integrated solution. This enabled us to capture around 15% market share of the Stock Connect daily north-bound trading volumes.

'But the focus should not be on aggregate quota usage or trading turnover, because Stock Connect is much bigger than that: it's a catalyst, and a model, for the future,' defended Charles Li, CEO of the Hong Kong Stock Exchange, on the first anniversary of the scheme.[37]

The Stock Connect was an unusual and innovative framework, established through the close cooperation and consultation of the Shanghai and Hong Kong stock exchanges, securities regulators, industry experts and participants. While it was not a surprise that the Hong Kong Stock Exchange regularly engaged the industry in the process, the Shanghai Stock Exchange very much did its part too. The trading rules and regulations, including the clarification of custodian arrangements and beneficial-ownership issues, along with trading infrastructure and system, continue to be reviewed and improved for market efficiency and certainty.

An extension of the programme, the Shenzhen-Hong Kong Stock Connect, was also launched and went live on 5 December 2016 to allow access to mainland companies listed on the Shenzhen Stock Exchange.

Another significant market-changing development was the China-Hong Kong Mutual Recognition of Funds (MRF) scheme, under

37 *Shanghai-HK Stock Connect 'a model' for the future*, 17 November 2015, *China Daily*.

which retail funds approved by the home securities regulator that would meet relevant eligibility requirements could apply to the regulator of the other market for a public offer to the investors in that host market. The MRF scheme, which regulators first started discussing in 2012, was hailed as a game-changer by the industry by opening up the mainland retail market for direct access to international investment funds domiciled in Hong Kong without establishing a local presence. It was also significant in bringing mainland funds to Hong Kong and potentially beyond, giving international investors first-hand and direct access to domestic mainland securities investment funds, and thereby, access to the investment capability of mainland investment managers in a broader range of strategies and sector focus.

The scheme was announced through a mutual cooperation memorandum between the CSRC and the Hong Kong SFC in July 2015. The first batch of seven funds, three north-bound and four south-bound funds, were approved to start distribution in December. As of October 2016, the number of approved north-bound funds was increased to six and south-bound funds to forty-eight.

Following a slow start in January, the sales figures were getting more and more encouraging each month. As at the end of October 2016, the six north-bound MRF funds from BOCHK Asset Management, Hang Seng Asset Management, JP Morgan Asset Management, and Zeal Asset Management, raised RMB8.48 billion (US$1.22 billion) in aggregate in the first ten months of the year, according to data released by SAFE. JP Morgan accounted for close to 90% of the sales, notably from the very strong client demand of its Asian Total Return Bond Fund.

Hong Kong-based asset managers would need time to understand the MRF process and, more importantly, to develop new distribution partnerships in China - banks, securities houses, IFAs (independent financial advisors) and online platforms. Some of these channels, such as online platforms, were new to them. At the same time, these distributors in China would need to learn how to promote these north-bound MRF funds.

Conversely, there was muted interest from Hong Kong investors for south-bound funds, raising only RMB95.8 million (US$13.91 million) in aggregate over the ten months. The lack-lustre results were largely due to the low investor confidence following the collapse of the A-Share market in summer 2015, and the depreciation of the RMB throughout 2016.

The pace of opening up China's capital market continued in 2016 despite the summer rout of the A-Share market. In February, the PBOC took a giant step to open up the mainland interbank bond market to eligible foreign institutions including commercial banks and other financial institutions, fund managers and asset management institutions, and medium and long-term institutional investors. This gave international investors access to China's US$7 trillion of onshore bonds, the third largest in the world, which had so far been accessible on a limited basis by QFIIs and RQFIIs, or central banks and supranational institutions. Qualifying foreign investors would appoint interbank market settlement agents (which are de facto custodians) to register and establish trading and settlement accounts in order to participate. The strict quota system was replaced by a much simplified registration and filing system.

Previously, the QFII or RQFII could take between twelve to eighteen months to get quota approval. The change would cut through the cumbersome process. In addition, the scheme removed lock-up period and restrictions on the repatriation of funds - a constant source of complaint among QFII/RQFII investors.

BNP Paribas (China) Ltd, a locally-incorporated bank of the Group, was one of the only four foreign banks that had obtained the Type-A license for acting as a settlement agent for Chinese interbank bond market. This presented another good business opportunity. In view of the previous successfully experience, we joined efforts with Global Markets to offer clients an end-to-end execution to settlement and custody solution. The Implementation Measures were announced in May, but investors took a measured pace to invest in the market as the RMB currency was under a lot of depreciation pressure due to capital flights. Nonetheless, our filing for five funds managed by Aberdeen Asset Management was successfully accepted by the PBOC, representing the first UCITS funds investing in the market through this new initiative.

With the RMB being officially included in the IMF's SDR currency basket starting from October 2016, many central banks around the world would have to include RMB denominated bonds as part of their foreign reserves investment. Consideration of inclusion of the Chinese interbank bonds in the JP Morgan, Citibank or Barclays global bond indices would be a matter of time.

At the same time, CSRC and SAFE also announced new foreign-exchange rules for the QFII regime that greatly enhanced flexibility in quotas, such that they would be given based on needs or the size of assets under management or specific needs, subject to a maximum limit of US$5 billion per QFII. The new QFII rules would now match the liquidity for open-ended funds to those under RQFII, allowing daily liquidity.

Notwithstanding some uncertainties, these were huge steps that further opened up the market and would offer valuable investment opportunities to the global investment community not previously available. The interbank bond market would be almost completely open, and together with Shanghai and soon Shenzhen Stock Connect, about 85% of the country's securities market would be accessible to foreign investors without the need for quota application and approval, which ten years ago was simply unimaginable.

China access programmes; Source: BNP Paribas

The Chinese agenda of RMB internationalisation has created many new opportunities to asset managers and custodians, but at the same time the industry's ability and capacity to cope with the pace of the development has been put to test.

A very significant development in this process since the global financial crisis is that Chinese financial institutions are at the forefront of many of these initiatives, unlike in the previous decade or before, during which foreign players with their global expertise were pivotal to the initial launches. This reflects the maturing of Chinese financial institutions and the role they are entrusted with in China's RMB internationalisation strategy. Many of them are already very successful in China and would want to tap into opportunities outside China arising from the RMB internationalisation process. Hong Kong is the platform for Chinese fund managers and brokers taking the first step to embark on their *Go-Global* strategy following the footsteps of Chinese insurers and banks. A number of fund managers such as Harvest Fund Management, GF Fund Management and E-Fund Management are venturing into New York and London for distributing their products in their next step to go global, while BOC, International & Commercial Bank of China (ICBC) and China Construction Bank (CCB) are actively building their custodian network outside China.

It will still be some way before any of the Chinese managers or custodian banks establish their brand name and credibility in overseas markets. But with a strong growing fund-management market at home and the fast-rising economic prowess of China, will it be too long before we see a Chinese player leap into the top league in the world?

Appendix: RMB Internationalisation Milestones

2002

- Domestic Securities Investment by Qualified Foreign Institutional Investor (QFII regulation) was announced in November, allowing foreign investors to access mainland stock markets (A-Shares).

2003

- People's Bank of China (PBOC) designated Bank of China Hong Kong as RMB clearing and settlement bank

2004

- RMB deposits were allowed in Hong Kong, which became the first offshore RMB centre.

2006

- The Qualified Domestic Institutional Investor (QDII) scheme was announced in April, allowing Chinese institutions and residents to entrust Chinese commercial banks to invest in financial products overseas.

2007

- Establishment of the Offshore RMB bond, the 'dim-sum' bonds market, which has been doubling in size each year since 2008.

2008

- Implementation of Cross-Border Trade RMB Settlement Pilot Project in December. The first Bilateral Swap Agreement was signed with South Korea.

2009

- A pilot trade scheme was introduced for five major Chinese trading cities (Dongguan, Guangzhou, Shanghai, Shenzhen and Zhuhai), ASEAN countries, Hong Kong and Macau, enabling RMB to be used to settle trade payments for the first time

2010

- PBOC issued policy in August to allow Central Bank, RMB Offshore Clearing Banks and Offshore Participating Bank to invest the excess RMB in debt securities, in onshore Interbank Bond Market.

- China and Russia began trading in their own currencies in November, abandoning the US Dollar as the medium of exchange in bilateral trade. This was followed by Japan in December 2011.

2011

- China in October published rules for outbound direct investment (ODI) and foreign direct investment (FDI) enabling RMB capital to flow more freely.

- PBOC released on 31 December the Announcement of the People's Bank of China Concerning the Implementation of Measures for the Pilot Program of Allowing Fund Management Companies and Securities Companies Approved as Renminbi Qualified Foreign Institutional Investors (RQFII) to Invest in Domestic Securities Market.

2013

- RMB overtook the Euro in December to become the second-most-used currency in global trade finance after the US Dollar, according to the Society for Worldwide Interbank Financial Telecommunication (SWIFT).

2014

- China Securities Regulatory Commission (CSRC) and the Securities & Futures Commission of Hong Kong (SFC) announced in April a joint statement of a trial trading program known as Shanghai-Hong Kong Stock Connect, allowing two-way cross-market stock investment by qualified Mainland Chinese and Hong Kong investors.

- Shanghai Free Trade Zone materialised and SAFE issued Circular 36 in July to extend benefits to foreign-invested enterprises (FIEs) in sixteen other industrial parks and economic zones.

- Shanghai-Hong Kong Stock Connect debuted in November with a bang, hitting its RMB13 billion one-day trading cap at 13:57 HK time - less than five hours after markets opened

2015

- CSRC and SFC in May announced Mutual Recognition of Funds enabling approved Hong Kong domiciled mutual funds to be distributed in Mainland China and vice versa

- PBoC in July opened up the US$5.7 trillion interbank bond market to foreign Central Banks, Sovereign Wealth Funds and supranational financial institutions.

- China International Payments System (CIPS) was launched in October as an alternative to SWIFT.

- The IMF confirmed in November the inclusion of the RMB in its Special Drawing Rights (SDR) basket starting from October 2016.

2016

- PBOC in February lifted the barrier into the China Interbank Bond market (CIBM), the world's third largest credit market (US$7 trillion). The Implementation Rules for Foreign Investors to Access the Chinese Interbank Bond Market was announced in May.

- SAFE in February announced new rules on how the base investment quota for QFII was determined and the filing procedure that replaced the previous approval process. The inward remittance deadline was abolished and the lock-up period was also reduced to allow earlier repatriation of invested funds.

- Shenzhen-Hong Kong Stock Connect went live on 5 December.

Source:

Internationalisation of the Renminbi: Major Milestones, Wikipedia; *RMB Internationlisation: The Story So Far*, HSBC

22. The A-Share Market Rout

2015 saw a dramatic boom-and-bust of the Chinese stock market that gripped the nerves of the whole world.

From June 2014 to June 2015, stock prices increased by more than 150% on the Shanghai Exchange, and even more on the Shenzhen Stock Exchange and the Shenzhen ChiNext, hitting a seven-year peak. The rise was fueled by falling borrowing costs as the central bank loosened monetary policy, as well as by a switch away from property investment following a clampdown by the government on excessive lending by banks.

In early 2015, some analysts had already been warning that the dramatic rise in China's stock markets was driven by momentum rather than fundamentals and the stocks were looking wildly overvalued. However, many more were exhorting that this was merely the start of a bull market. An online commentary published in the *People's Daily* on 21 April entitled *What's a bubble? Tulips and Bitcoins are bubbles*,[38] mocked fears of a Chinese stock-market bubble and assured readers that continued gains would enjoy full support from China's grand development strategy and economic reforms. The commentary was quickly shared across the Web, accompanied, in some cases, by a cartoon of a bull ramming a giant arrow towards the sky.

Millions of retail investors flocked into the market with mass amounts of investments. In the three months from March to June 2015, a total of thirty-eight million new securities accounts were opened for investing in the stock market compared with nine million new accounts opened for the whole year in 2014. At the same time, many

38 *The Real Risk Behind China's Stock-Market Drama*, 15 July 2105, *The New Yorker*.

of the investments were leveraged using borrowed money from margin lending which was introduced since March 2010. At the peak of China's stock market, in mid-June 2015, the total amount of margin loans extended by Chinese brokerages to investors stood at RMB2.26 trillion.[39]

However, there was a lot more grey-market margin lending by shadow banks going on beyond the purview of regulators. Using small lenders, online lenders, trust companies or other sources, retail investors borrowed three to ten times their initial small stakes at high interest rates and invested the money in small- and mid-cap stocks with strong price movements. The effective leverage ratios involved were well above those available through normal margin lending.

Then a crash began with the bubble-burst on 12 June 2015. A third of the value of A-Shares on the Shanghai Stock Exchange was lost within one month, followed by major after-shocks occurring around 27 July and 24 August's Black Monday. The contagion effect was being felt globally. 'The sell-off in Chinese stocks in recent weeks makes the volatility in European and US indices look like a walk in the park,' commented a research director at Forex.com, the currency specialist firm.[40]

The Chinese authorities stepped in with various market operations to halt the sharp decline, including a crack-down on margin trading. The falling share prices triggered margin calls and investors had to offload their stock holdings or other assets to come up with the cash they needed, pushing the market further down. On 24 August, the market fell 8.48 percent, marking the largest fall since 2007. About 1,300 Chinese companies - almost half of the market - suspended dealings in their shares in a bid to arrest the frenzy of selling.

39 *China's Gray Market in Margin Lending Is Probably Massive*, 9 July 2015, *Bloomberg*.

40 *Why is China's stock market in crisis?* 8 July 2015, *The Guardian*.

Because so many of the investors in the market were private individuals, the government was acutely aware that deepening losses would risk denting the real economy, even leading to social unrest. The Chinese authorities ordered a curb on new share issues and enlisted a 'national' team of brokers and fund managers to buy massive amounts of shares to steady the stock market, backed by China's state-backed margin finance company, the China Securities Finance Corporation (CSFC) which had a direct line of liquidity from the central bank.

By the end of December 2015, the Chinese stock market had recovered from the shocks and outperformed the S&P for 2015. By the end of 2015, the Shanghai Composite Index was up 12.6% percent for the year even though still well below the highs of 12 June.

Many of the measures taken to prop up the market by the Chinese authorities during the summer rout of 2015 were highly controversial, and were seen by foreign investors as market meddling. China was certainly not the first country to try to prop up a falling stock market. The central banks of America, Europe and Asia had all bought shares after crashes and cut interest rates for broadly the same reasons. But the circumstances and the manner of the Chinese government's intervention made it an outlier with actions such as: halting the trading of thousands of stocks, banning major shareholders from selling, threatening to arrest the shorts, and pulling in hundreds of people from the industry for investigations. The government's actions have caused major concerns about its commitment and ability to transit to a market-driven economy for sustainable growth.

Notwithstanding the controversy and concern, at the centre of the dramatic rise and fall of the Chinese stock-market crisis was a core group of individual investors participating heavily in the market, known fondly as *Dama,* that caught the eyes of the world.

The word *Dama* (大妈) in Chinese literally means 'big mama'. It refers to a category of investors described by the *Wall Street Journal* as bargain-hunting middle-aged Chinese women who keep a tight grip on the family purse and an eagle eye on investing in gold, Bitcoins, properties, and stock markets with their aggressive herd-like behaviour. They had made the headlines a number of times over the past few years.

In mid-April 2013, when gold prices fell to a lower level, many Chinese *Damas* jumped at the chance for what they deemed a bargain. It was estimated that the *Dama* investors bought three hundred tonnes of gold worth RMB100 billion (US$16.4 billion), or some 10% of the world's annual production, in ten days, sweeping jewelry stores across the nation including Hong Kong, cleaning anything containing gold. The investment was so fast and large that investment banks such as Goldman Sachs, that had previously been shorting on gold, had to reverse their stance and the gold price soon stabilised. The *Wall Street Journal* reported the stunning news by spelling out the Chinese word *Dama* directly. However, the gold price has been falling since then and those *Dama* investors might take a long time to recoup their costs until the gold price recovers to US$1,360 an ounce.

Damas rushing to buy gold; Source: blog.sina.com

In 2013, Chinese *Damas* made their name once again by swallowing Bitcoin, the value of which surged by eighty-nine times to over US$1,000 in July since it was released three years ago. According to a Chinese Bitcoin exchange website, 40% of their VIP clients who bought and sold more than RMB10 million Bitcoins per day were Chinese *Damas*. Again, the price of Bitcoin had since dropped significantly as central banks around the world intervened to stop the unsubstantiated cyber value of Bitcoins.

These *Damas*, estimated by some Chinese media reports to number more than 100 million, did everything in groups. They entertained themselves in groups, danced in groups and travelled in groups. They even speculated on real estate and stocks in groups. Big data released by Internet financing company *wacai.com* in 2015 showed that per-capita investment amount of fifty-five-year-old or above females was 43% higher than overall per-capita investment and was nearly three times the per-capita investment of those born after 1980[41].

Damas enjoying a group square dance; Source: www.4006819989.com

41 *Chinese Dama favors internet financial products*, 1 December 2015, *People's Daily Online*

Deeply influenced by traditional culture, *Damas* worked hard and didn't enjoy a good life when they were young; they only tried their best to save money. Now their children had grown up, they had more free time and money to spend on their own life with retirement pensions.

They were often seen in stock brokerage houses, banks and property agencies, and they went about their investment decisions in much the same way as they bought clothes in shopping malls and food in the wet market.

Damas were careful in spending money and paid special attention to cost performance. Their love for gold was not influenced by the warnings of risks issued by analysts. They did not care whether the price went up or come down after they bought it because they wanted to pass it down to their daughters or daughters-in-law. 'Gold is forever gold, whether it appreciates or depreciates,' said Mrs. Yao, a *Dama* who bought some gold jewelry at a relatively higher price.[42]

They also showed their cautious attitude when they invested in overseas property markets. They saw a post on *WeChat* that RMB1 million (US$164,000) could buy much better houses abroad than in Beijing. Besides appreciation, they thought their children or grandchildren might be able to use the houses while studying or working abroad.

Chinese *Damas* have been closely watched, teased, ridiculed and written about over the past few years in the media. Their influence has gone beyond gold, Bitcoin, properties, and the stock market. They have become a cultural phenomenon in their own right, a figure of fun with their favourite pastime of dancing in public squares. They are the outcome of the fact that currently, in mainland China,

---

42 *Dama: China's secret weapon*, 10 December, 2013, http://www.sino-us.com/

financial literacy and professional private wealth management are very much under-developed.

Damas usually have a large amount of idle money after having saved throughout most of their lives. 'In a majority of families, women are the financial controllers,' said Ivan Li, a wealth manager who used to work at a China Merchants Bank branch in Shanghai's Huangpu district[43].

While their aggressive group-purchasing behaviour is fascinating, their investments have often been bottom-fishing typical of the group psychology of retail investors.

In future, there will be fewer such elderly women who like to invest but are financially illiterate, Li said. The market teaches them lessons and people will become more educated in wealth management.

But until the Chinese market matures to become much more institutionally driven, after Damas, there might be Dajies (**大姊**, big sisters) punting on the market in droves when the next bubble develops.

43 *Why China's women are being pursued by wealth managers and property agents*, 17 December 2015, *South China Morning Post*.

Epilogue

The idea of writing a book on the custody industry came out of lunch with a journalist from the *South China Morning Post* in April 2015 together with Michelle Toy and Lilian Goh, my marketing and communications colleagues at BNP Paribas.

The journalist had been with *South China Morning Post* for more than two decades covering business news. Like most journalists working in the general media, custody was not a subject matter she knew in depth. But the conversation turned out to be very interactive and interesting for all of us around the table. We spent almost the entire lunch sharing stories about the evolution of the financial market and the investment-management industry in Hong Kong and the region. I shared stories that I had come across over my years working as a custodian - the other side of the coin. And while I talked she would ask me to explain terms such as 'safekeeping', 'coupon payments', 'scrip', 'physical delivery', etc. and everyone was amused by the stories behind them. At the end of the lunch, she suggested that I should write a book and share the stories.

Writing a book was not on my bucket list before this. I chewed on the suggestion and agreed that it would be a good idea to share the story of Asia's finance industry over the past few decades from the perspective of a custodian. There are many episodes and events that I have witnessed and gone through with other professionals in the industry that are worth passing on as part of a history that few others have written on.

I have not written a book before and I would not know whether any publisher would be interested in it but, in any case, I went ahead. It took me twelve months to complete the first draft manuscript because I could only work on it after a full day's work and when I was not on trips. It was quite a venture but was definitely a lot easier than writing my thesis for MBA graduation back in 1981. The big difference is the Internet, which is a wonderful tool for searching out information in addition to what I have in the books, magazine articles, and notes that I have collected from my work over the years.

The first eight chapters of the book trace the global historical evolution of securities trading, settlement and custody functions and market infrastructure while they developed in Asia. The remaining chapters delineate the major events over the past three decades and their impact on the evolution and transformation of the region's financial industry.

As I researched on this book and tried to put my thoughts in writing, it became very evident how much the industry has evolved to where it is today as an outcome in response to a host of market boom-and-bust cycles during its development. The process was like joining the dots. It is absolutely amazing to rediscover once again how the industry has managed to survive and regenerate itself through the various financial, technological, economic, social, and regulatory disruptions, which mark the volatile history of financial-market development in the region over the past three decades.

It was at the same time a humbling experience. I realised through the process the limits of my knowledge even though I have been working in the industry for so long. It was only through looking back and with the benefit of hindsight that I gained a better understanding of these complex events.

Most of the time, out of the limelight, many professionals in the custody industry have been working with great dedication to overcome big and small crises, to solve complex issues and come up with innovations to meet new investment challenges. They have helped make the industry stronger and more robust and helped it to evolve to where it is today.

We don't know who we are unless we know where we have come from. I hope this book will make useful and interesting reading for those currently working in the industry as well as those joining in the future - to help them have a better understanding of the journey before and to foster new ideas to define the future.

This is my small recompense to an industry which has given me such an amazing and rewarding experience of work for a very long and important part of my career and my life.

At the time of writing this book, both KK Tse and Leow Chong-Jin have retired from the industry. Laurence Bailey and I are stepping down at the beginning of 2016 to transition for retirement. This marks the phasing-out of the first generation of home-grown pioneers of the industry in the region.

The future belongs to the tens of thousands of talented professionals in the industry working incessantly day in and day out to define its path in meeting the evolving opportunities and challenges in the region.

INDEX

T

About the Author

Lawrence Au is a seasoned professional who has been at the forefront of Asia's financial industry for more than thirty years. A pioneer and thought leader in the securities services area, he has been instrumental in building several custodian banks' businesses in the region. Under his stewardship as the Asia Pacific head with BNP Paribas Securities Services and Northern Trust, he took the custody franchise of the two banks off the ground to become a leading service provider in the market.

Lawrence frequently speaks at conferences and features in industry publications, and was named Custodian Leader of the Year 2012 by Asia Asset Management and Custodian Banker of the Year 2013 by The Asset. He was presented Life-time Achievement Award by Asia Asset Management in 2016.

www.facebook.com/LawrenceAuAuthor/
http://linkedin.com/in/lawrence-au-598a5b38

About the Author

Made in the USA
Monee, IL
04 November 2026

67384328R00138